D1457141

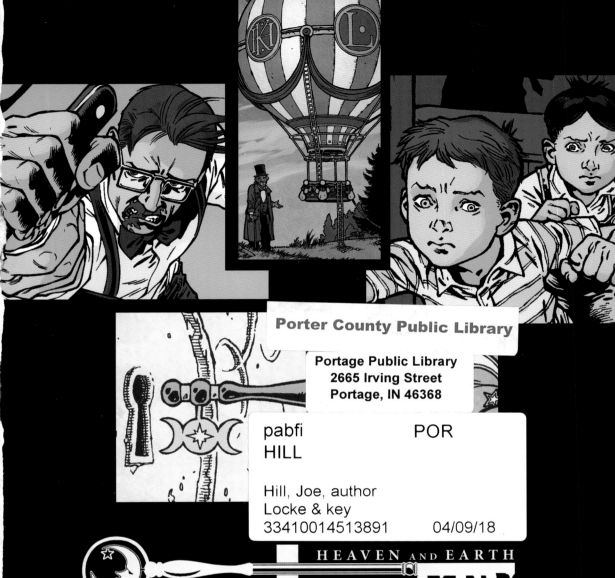

HEAVEN AND EARTH

LOCKE & KEY

WRITTEN BY
JOE HILL

ART BY
GABRIEL RODRIGUEZ

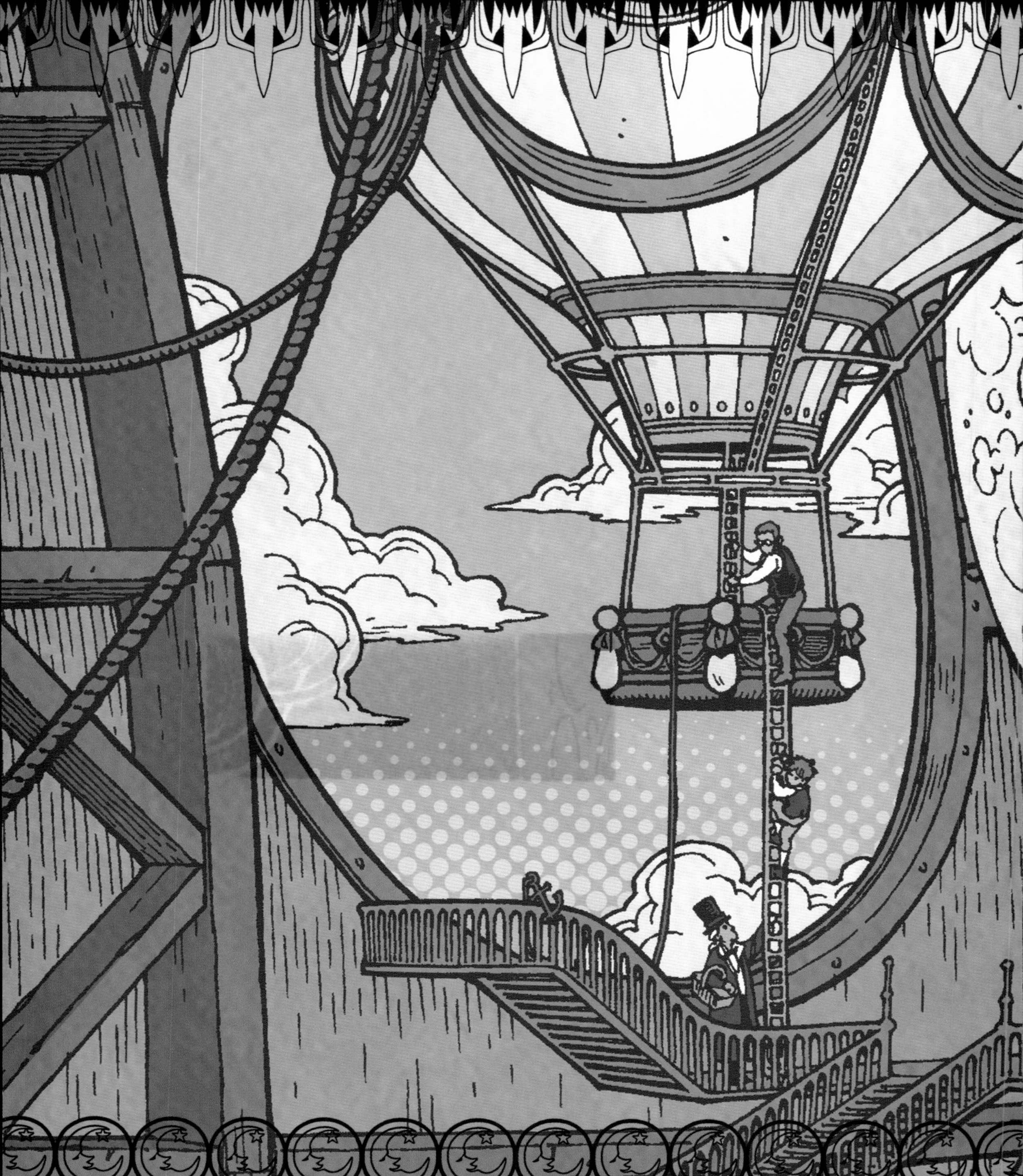

Locke & Key created by Joe Hill and Gabriel Rodriguez
Follow Joe Hill on Twitter @joe_hill • Follow Gabriel Rodriguez on Twitter @GR_comics

ISBN: 978-1-68405-181-6
For international rights, contact licensing@idwpublishing.com
20 19 18 17 1 2 3 4

IDW
www.IDWPUBLISHING.com

Ted Adams, CEO & Publisher • **Greg Goldstein**, President & COO • **Robbie Robbins**, EVP/Sr. Graphic Artist • **Chris Ryall**, Chief Creative Officer • **David Hedgecock**, Editor-in-Chief • **Laurie Windrow**, Senior Vice President of Sales & Marketing • **Matthew Ruzicka**, CPA, Chief Financial Officer • **Lorelei Bunjes**, VP of Digital Services • **Jerry Bennington**, VP of New Product Development

Facebook: **facebook.com/idwpublishing** • Twitter: **@idwpublishing** • YouTube: **youtube.com/idwpublishing**
Tumblr: **tumblr.idwpublishing.com** • Instagram: **instagram.com/idwpublishing**

Originally published as LOCKE & KEY: GUIDE TO THE KNOWN KEYS and LOCKE & KEY: GRINDHOUSE.

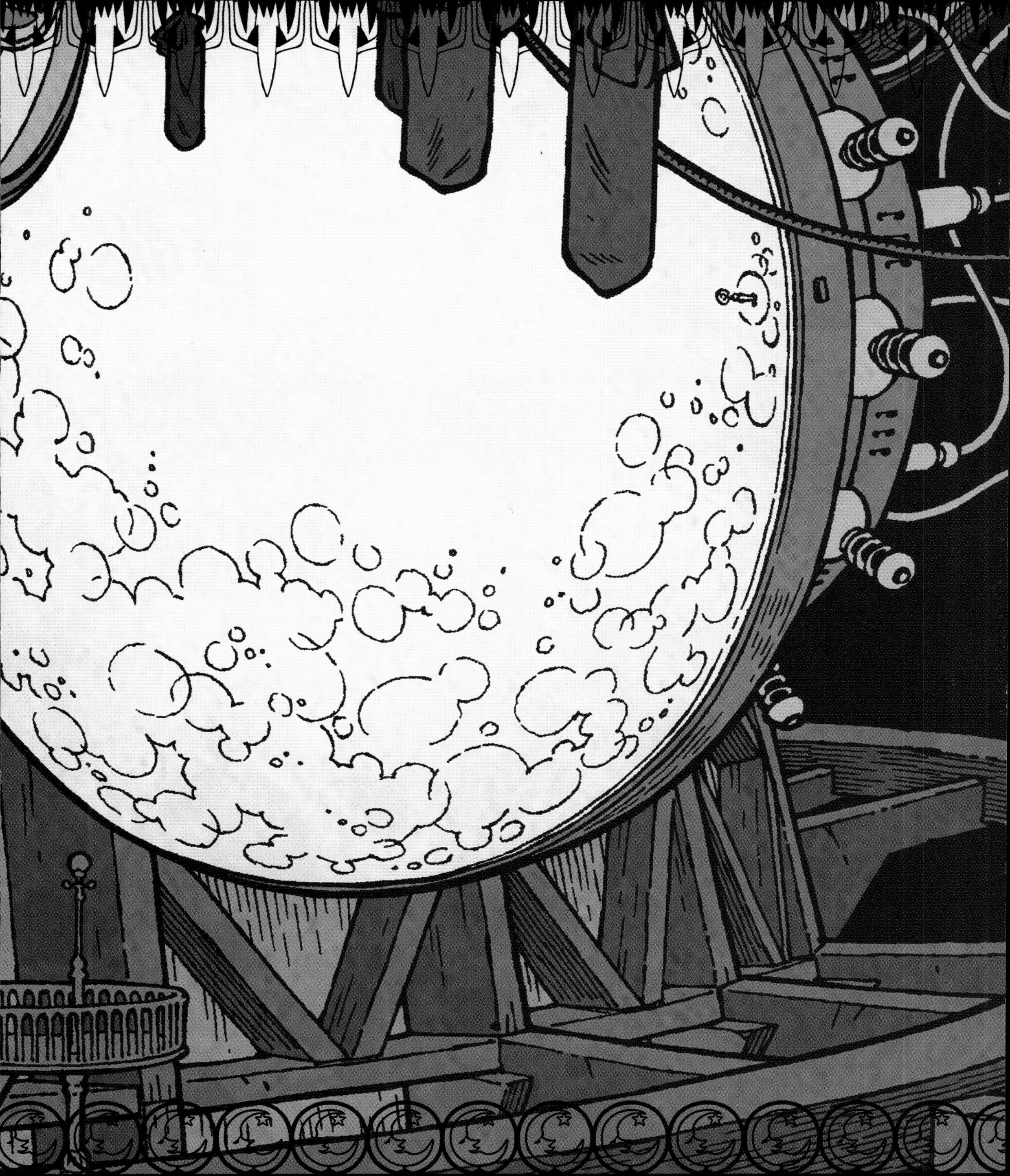

Written by: Joe Hill • Art by: Gabríel Rodriguez

Colors by: Jay Fotos • Letters by: Robbie Robbins

Series Edited by: Chris Ryall • Collection Edited by: Justin Eisinger

Collection Designed by: Robbie Robbins • Publisher: Ted Adams

TABLE OF CONTENTS

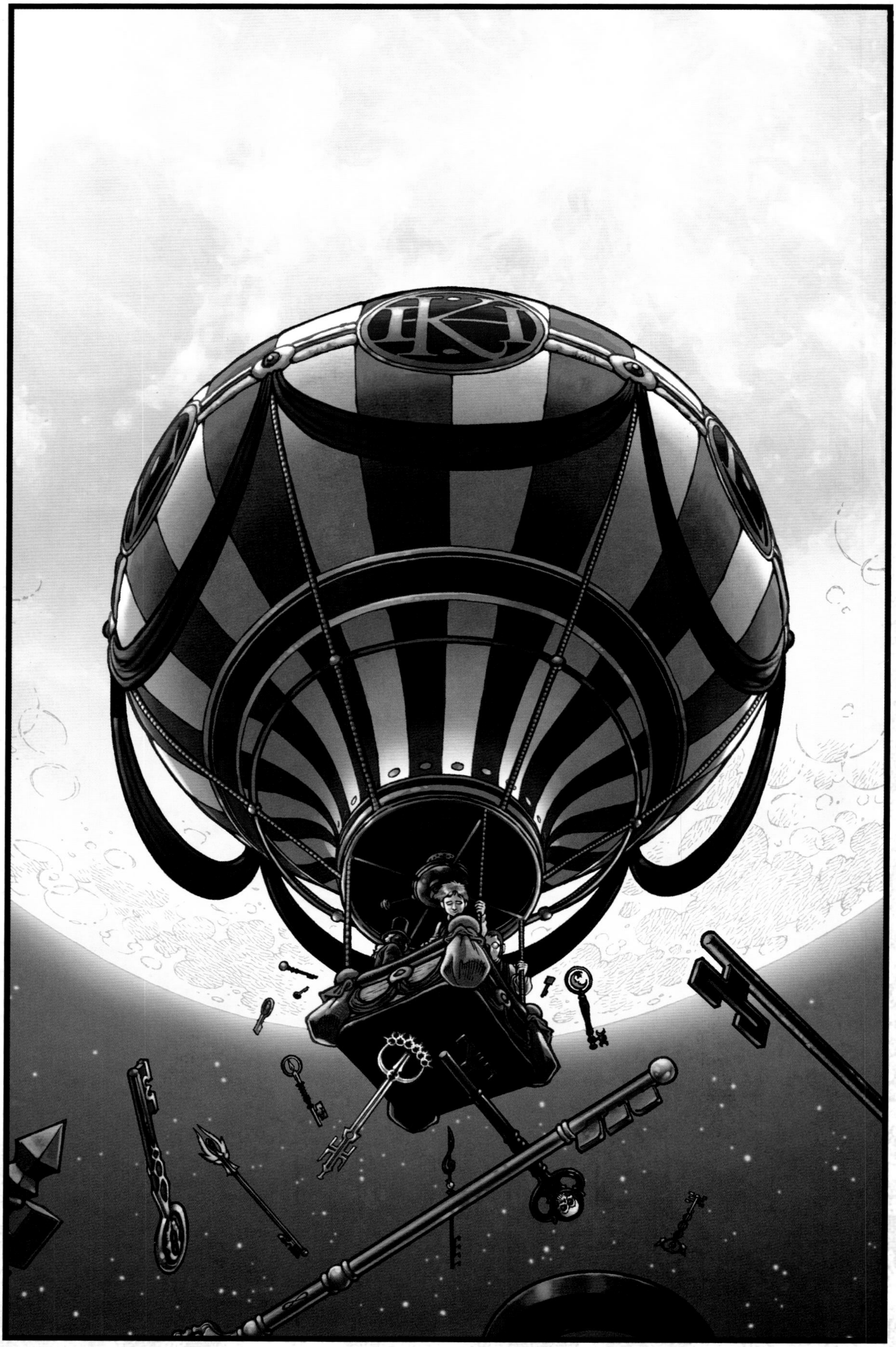

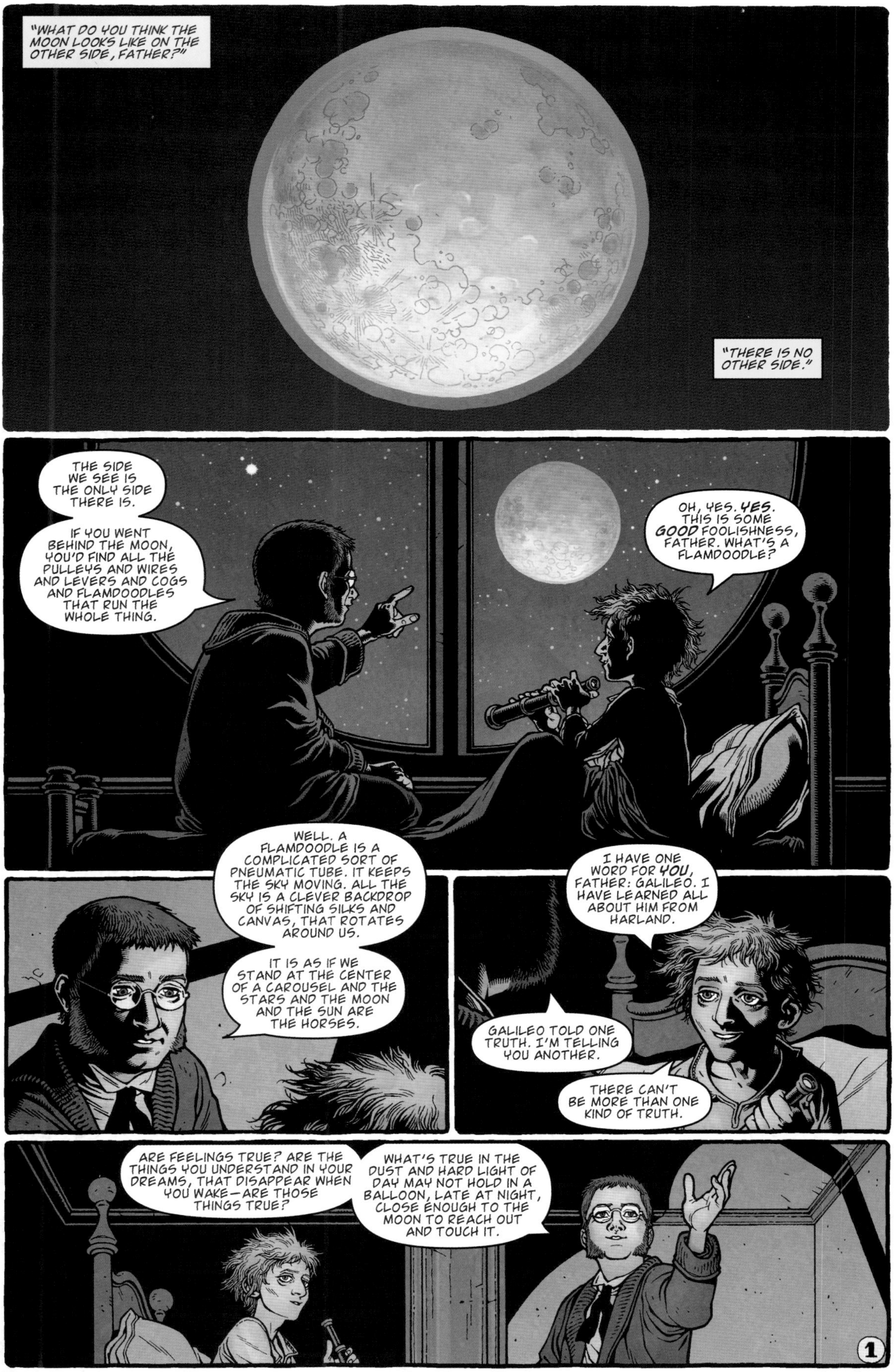
"WHAT DO YOU THINK THE MOON LOOKS LIKE ON THE OTHER SIDE, FATHER?"
"THERE IS NO OTHER SIDE."
THE SIDE WE SEE IS THE ONLY SIDE THERE IS.
IF YOU WENT BEHIND THE MOON, YOU'D FIND ALL THE PULLEYS AND WIRES AND LEVERS AND COGS AND FLAMDOODLES THAT RUN THE WHOLE THING.
OH, YES. **YES**. THIS IS SOME **GOOD** FOOLISHNESS, FATHER. WHAT'S A FLAMDOODLE?
WELL. A FLAMDOODLE IS A COMPLICATED SORT OF PNEUMATIC TUBE. IT KEEPS THE SKY MOVING. ALL THE SKY IS A CLEVER BACKDROP OF SHIFTING SILKS AND CANVAS, THAT ROTATES AROUND US.
IT IS AS IF WE STAND AT THE CENTER OF A CAROUSEL AND THE STARS AND THE MOON AND THE SUN ARE THE HORSES.
I HAVE ONE WORD FOR **YOU**, FATHER: GALILEO. I HAVE LEARNED ALL ABOUT HIM FROM HARLAND.
GALILEO TOLD ONE TRUTH. I'M TELLING YOU ANOTHER.
THERE CAN'T BE MORE THAN ONE KIND OF TRUTH.
ARE FEELINGS TRUE? ARE THE THINGS YOU UNDERSTAND IN YOUR DREAMS, THAT DISAPPEAR WHEN YOU WAKE—ARE THOSE THINGS TRUE?
WHAT'S TRUE IN THE DUST AND HARD LIGHT OF DAY MAY NOT HOLD IN A BALLOON, LATE AT NIGHT, CLOSE ENOUGH TO THE MOON TO REACH OUT AND TOUCH IT.
1

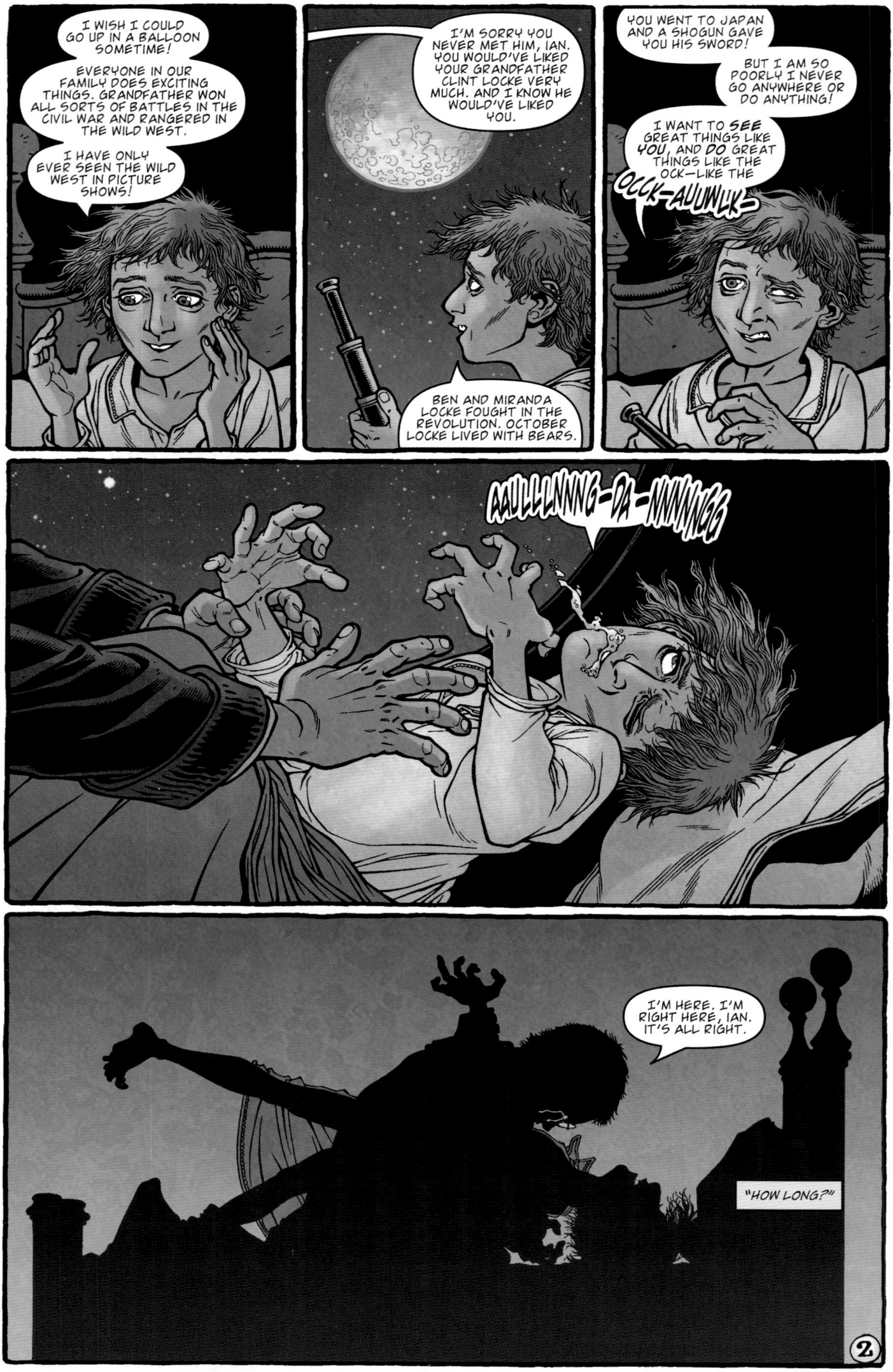
I WISH I COULD GO UP IN A BALLOON SOMETIME!
EVERYONE IN OUR FAMILY DOES EXCITING THINGS. GRANDFATHER WON ALL SORTS OF BATTLES IN THE CIVIL WAR AND RANGERED IN THE WILD WEST.
I HAVE ONLY EVER SEEN THE WILD WEST IN PICTURE SHOWS!
I'M SORRY YOU NEVER MET HIM, IAN. YOU WOULD'VE LIKED YOUR GRANDFATHER CLINT LOCKE VERY MUCH. AND I KNOW HE WOULD'VE LIKED YOU.
BEN AND MIRANDA LOCKE FOUGHT IN THE REVOLUTION. OCTOBER LOCKE LIVED WITH BEARS.
YOU WENT TO JAPAN AND A SHOGUN GAVE YOU HIS SWORD!
BUT I AM SO POORLY I NEVER GO ANYWHERE OR DO ANYTHING!
I WANT TO SEE GREAT THINGS LIKE YOU, AND DO GREAT THINGS LIKE THE OCK—LIKE THE
OCCK-AUUWLK-
AAULLLNNG-DA-NNNNGG
I'M HERE. I'M RIGHT HERE, IAN. IT'S ALL RIGHT.
"HOW LONG?"
2

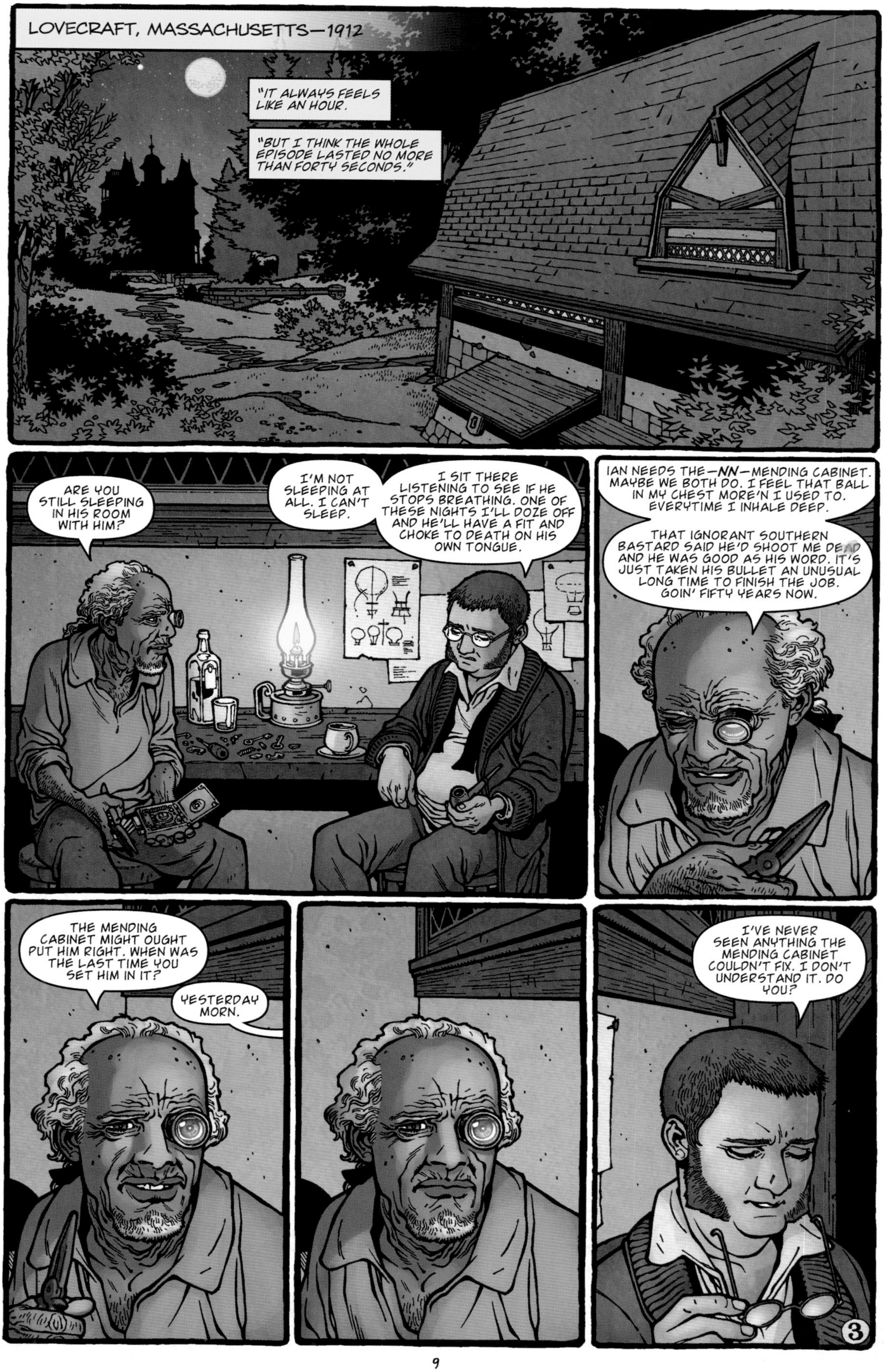
LOVECRAFT, MASSACHUSETTS—1912
"IT ALWAYS FEELS LIKE AN HOUR.
"BUT I THINK THE WHOLE EPISODE LASTED NO MORE THAN FORTY SECONDS."
ARE YOU STILL SLEEPING IN HIS ROOM WITH HIM?
I'M NOT SLEEPING AT ALL. I CAN'T SLEEP.
I SIT THERE LISTENING TO SEE IF HE STOPS BREATHING. ONE OF THESE NIGHTS I'LL DOZE OFF AND HE'LL HAVE A FIT AND CHOKE TO DEATH ON HIS OWN TONGUE.
IAN NEEDS THE—NN—MENDING CABINET. MAYBE WE BOTH DO. I FEEL THAT BALL IN MY CHEST MORE'N I USED TO. EVERYTIME I INHALE DEEP.
THAT IGNORANT SOUTHERN BASTARD SAID HE'D SHOOT ME DEAD AND HE WAS GOOD AS HIS WORD. IT'S JUST TAKEN HIS BULLET AN UNUSUAL LONG TIME TO FINISH THE JOB. GOIN' FIFTY YEARS NOW.
THE MENDING CABINET MIGHT OUGHT PUT HIM RIGHT. WHEN WAS THE LAST TIME YOU SET HIM IN IT?
YESTERDAY MORN.
I'VE NEVER SEEN ANYTHING THE MENDING CABINET COULDN'T FIX. I DON'T UNDERSTAND IT. DO YOU?
3

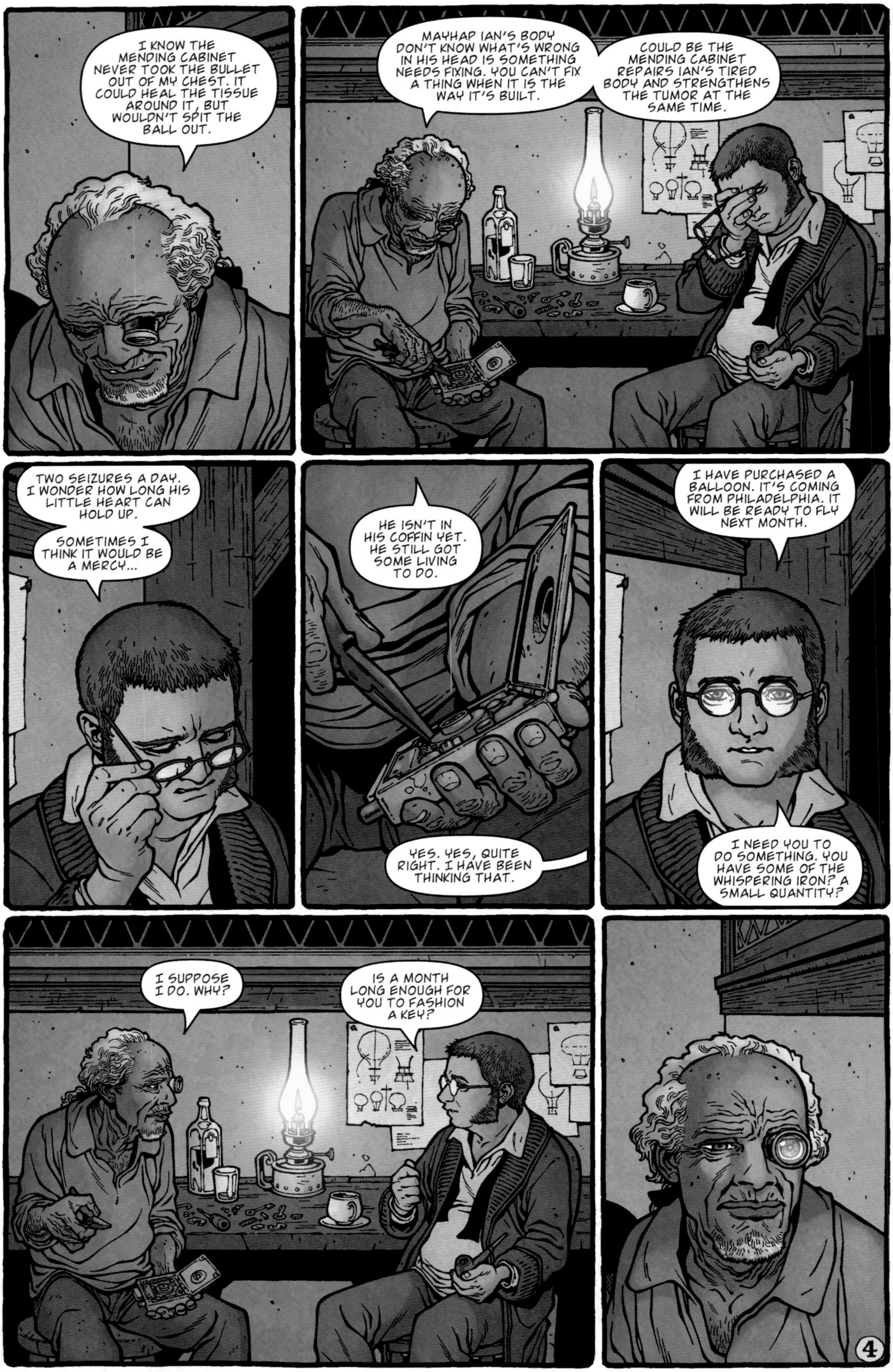
I KNOW THE MENDING CABINET NEVER TOOK THE BULLET OUT OF MY CHEST. IT COULD HEAL THE TISSUE AROUND IT, BUT WOULDN'T SPIT THE BALL OUT.
MAYHAP IAN'S BODY DON'T KNOW WHAT'S WRONG IN HIS HEAD IS SOMETHING NEEDS FIXING. YOU CAN'T FIX A THING WHEN IT IS THE WAY IT'S BUILT.
COULD BE THE MENDING CABINET REPAIRS IAN'S TIRED BODY AND STRENGTHENS THE TUMOR AT THE SAME TIME.
TWO SEIZURES A DAY. I WONDER HOW LONG HIS LITTLE HEART CAN HOLD UP.
SOMETIMES I THINK IT WOULD BE A MERCY...
HE ISN'T IN HIS COFFIN YET. HE STILL GOT SOME LIVING TO DO.
YES. YES, QUITE RIGHT. I HAVE BEEN THINKING THAT.
I HAVE PURCHASED A BALLOON. IT'S COMING FROM PHILADELPHIA. IT WILL BE READY TO FLY NEXT MONTH.
I NEED YOU TO DO SOMETHING. YOU HAVE SOME OF THE WHISPERING IRON? A SMALL QUANTITY?
I SUPPOSE I DO. WHY?
IS A MONTH LONG ENOUGH FOR YOU TO FASHION A KEY?
4

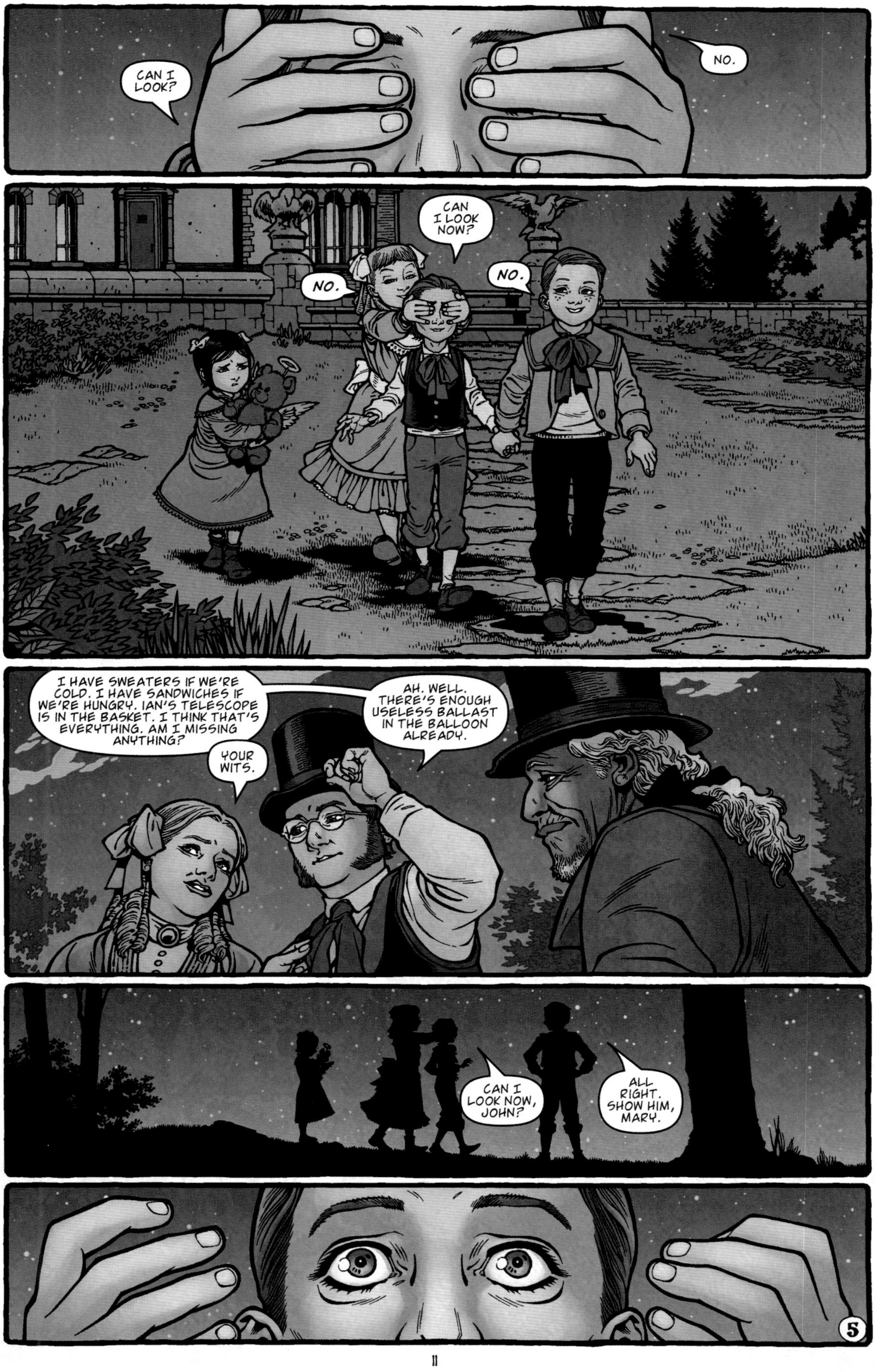
CAN I LOOK?
NO.
CAN I LOOK NOW?
NO.
NO.
I HAVE SWEATERS IF WE'RE COLD. I HAVE SANDWICHES IF WE'RE HUNGRY. IAN'S TELESCOPE IS IN THE BASKET. I THINK THAT'S EVERYTHING. AM I MISSING ANYTHING?
YOUR WITS.
AH. WELL. THERE'S ENOUGH USELESS BALLAST IN THE BALLOON ALREADY.
CAN I LOOK NOW, JOHN?
ALL RIGHT. SHOW HIM, MARY.
5

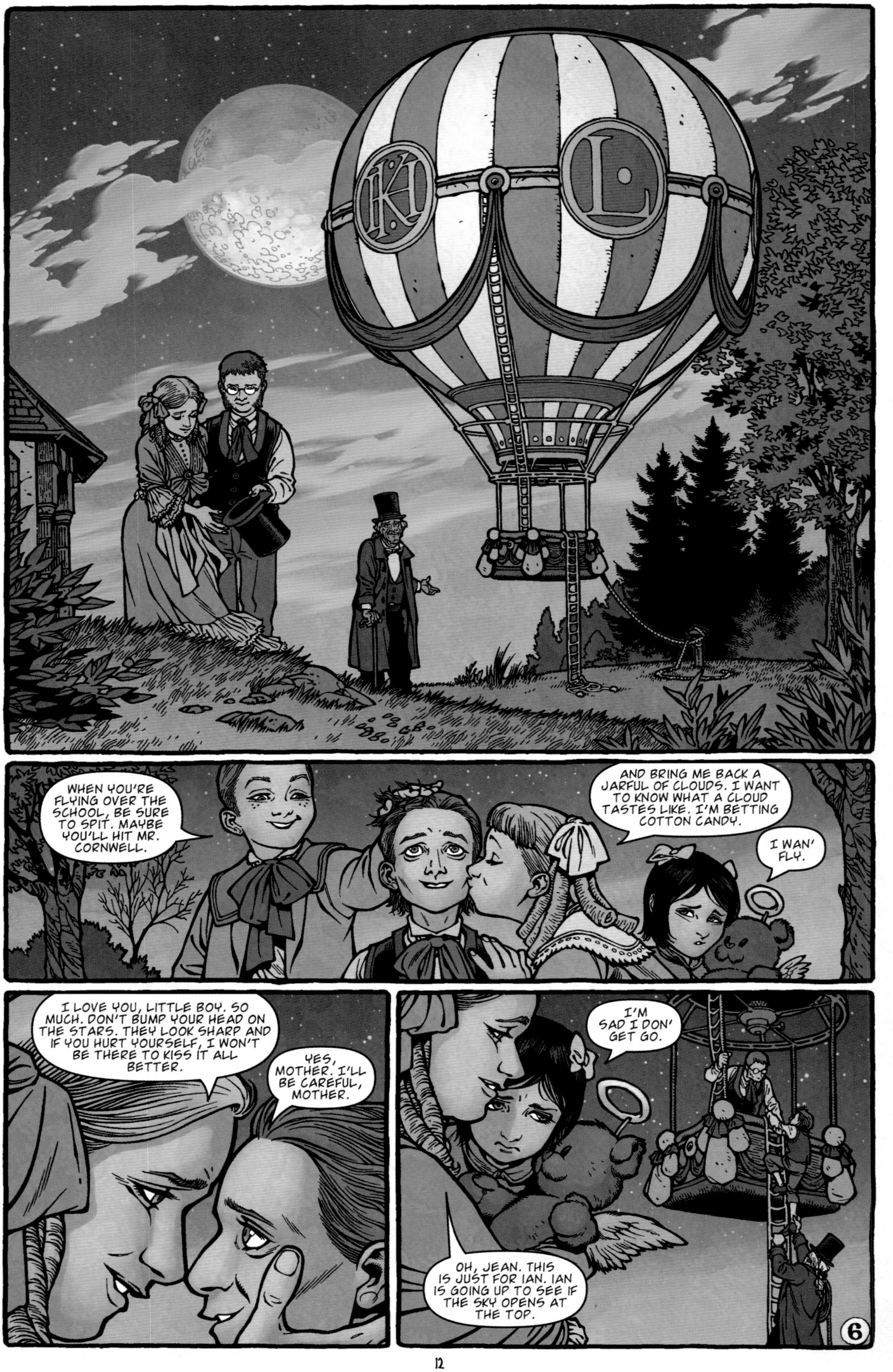
WHEN YOU'RE FLYING OVER THE SCHOOL, BE SURE TO SPIT. MAYBE YOU'LL HIT MR. CORNWELL.
AND BRING ME BACK A JARFUL OF CLOUDS. I WANT TO KNOW WHAT A CLOUD TASTES LIKE. I'M BETTING COTTON CANDY.
I WAN' FLY.
I LOVE YOU, LITTLE BOY. SO MUCH. DON'T BUMP YOUR HEAD ON THE STARS. THEY LOOK SHARP AND IF YOU HURT YOURSELF, I WON'T BE THERE TO KISS IT ALL BETTER.
YES, MOTHER. I'LL BE CAREFUL, MOTHER.
I'M SAD I DON' GET GO.
OH, JEAN. THIS IS JUST FOR IAN. IAN IS GOING UP TO SEE IF THE SKY OPENS AT THE TOP.
6

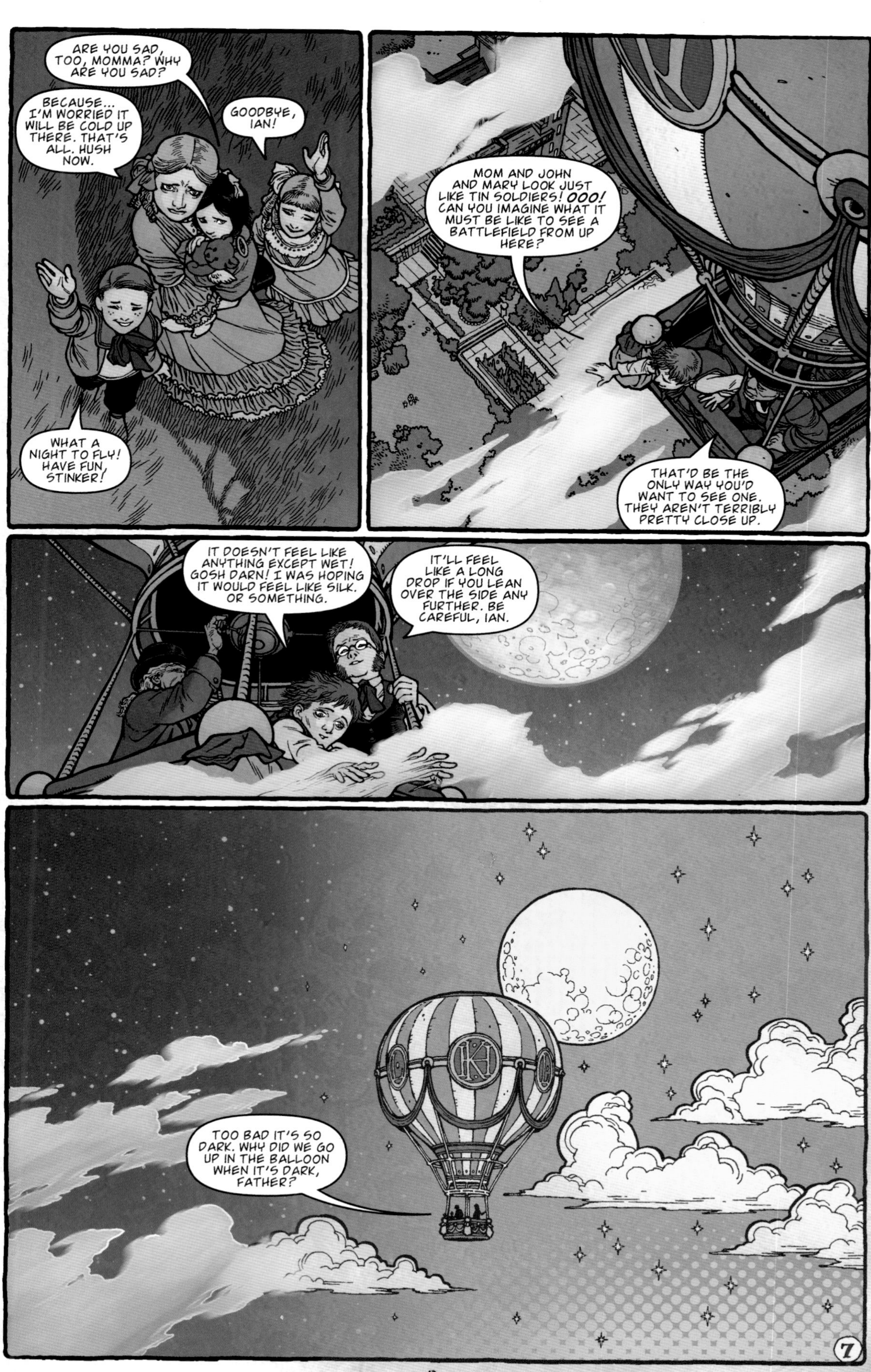
ARE YOU SAD, TOO, MOMMA? WHY ARE YOU SAD?
BECAUSE... I'M WORRIED IT WILL BE COLD UP THERE. THAT'S ALL. HUSH NOW.
GOODBYE, IAN!
WHAT A NIGHT TO FLY! HAVE FUN, STINKER!
MOM AND JOHN AND MARY LOOK JUST LIKE TIN SOLDIERS! OOO! CAN YOU IMAGINE WHAT IT MUST BE LIKE TO SEE A BATTLEFIELD FROM UP HERE?
THAT'D BE THE ONLY WAY YOU'D WANT TO SEE ONE. THEY AREN'T TERRIBLY PRETTY CLOSE UP.
IT DOESN'T FEEL LIKE ANYTHING EXCEPT WET! GOSH DARN! I WAS HOPING IT WOULD FEEL LIKE SILK. OR SOMETHING.
IT'LL FEEL LIKE A LONG DROP IF YOU LEAN OVER THE SIDE ANY FURTHER. BE CAREFUL, IAN.
TOO BAD IT'S SO DARK. WHY DID WE GO UP IN THE BALLOON WHEN IT'S DARK, FATHER?
7

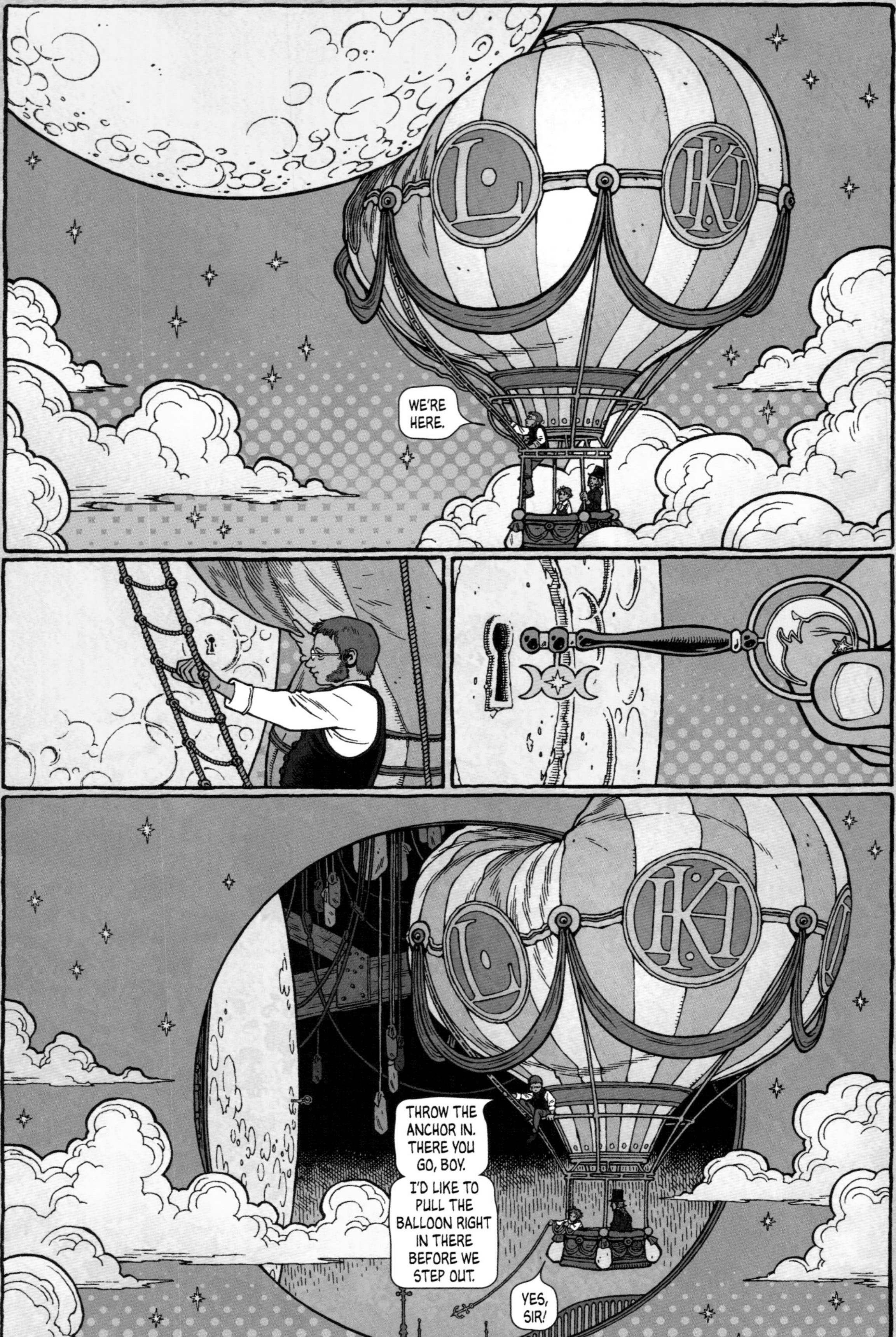
WE'RE HERE.
THROW THE ANCHOR IN. THERE YOU GO, BOY.
I'D LIKE TO PULL THE BALLOON RIGHT IN THERE BEFORE WE STEP OUT.
YES, SIR!
8

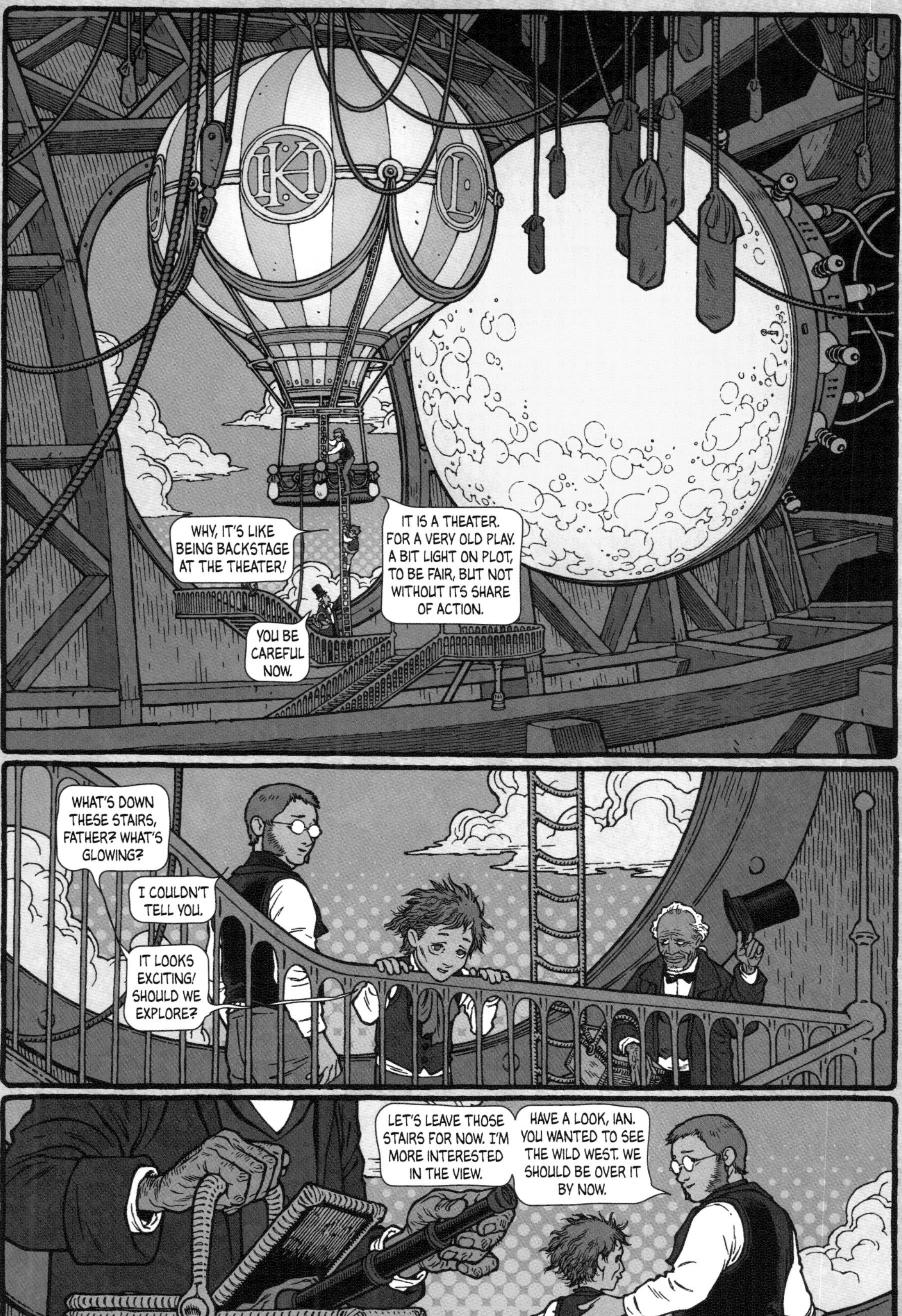
WHY, IT'S LIKE BEING BACKSTAGE AT THE THEATER!
IT IS A THEATER. FOR A VERY OLD PLAY. A BIT LIGHT ON PLOT, TO BE FAIR, BUT NOT WITHOUT ITS SHARE OF ACTION.
YOU BE CAREFUL NOW.
WHAT'S DOWN THESE STAIRS, FATHER? WHAT'S GLOWING?
I COULDN'T TELL YOU.
IT LOOKS EXCITING! SHOULD WE EXPLORE?
LET'S LEAVE THOSE STAIRS FOR NOW. I'M MORE INTERESTED IN THE VIEW.
HAVE A LOOK, IAN. YOU WANTED TO SEE THE WILD WEST. WE SHOULD BE OVER IT BY NOW.
9

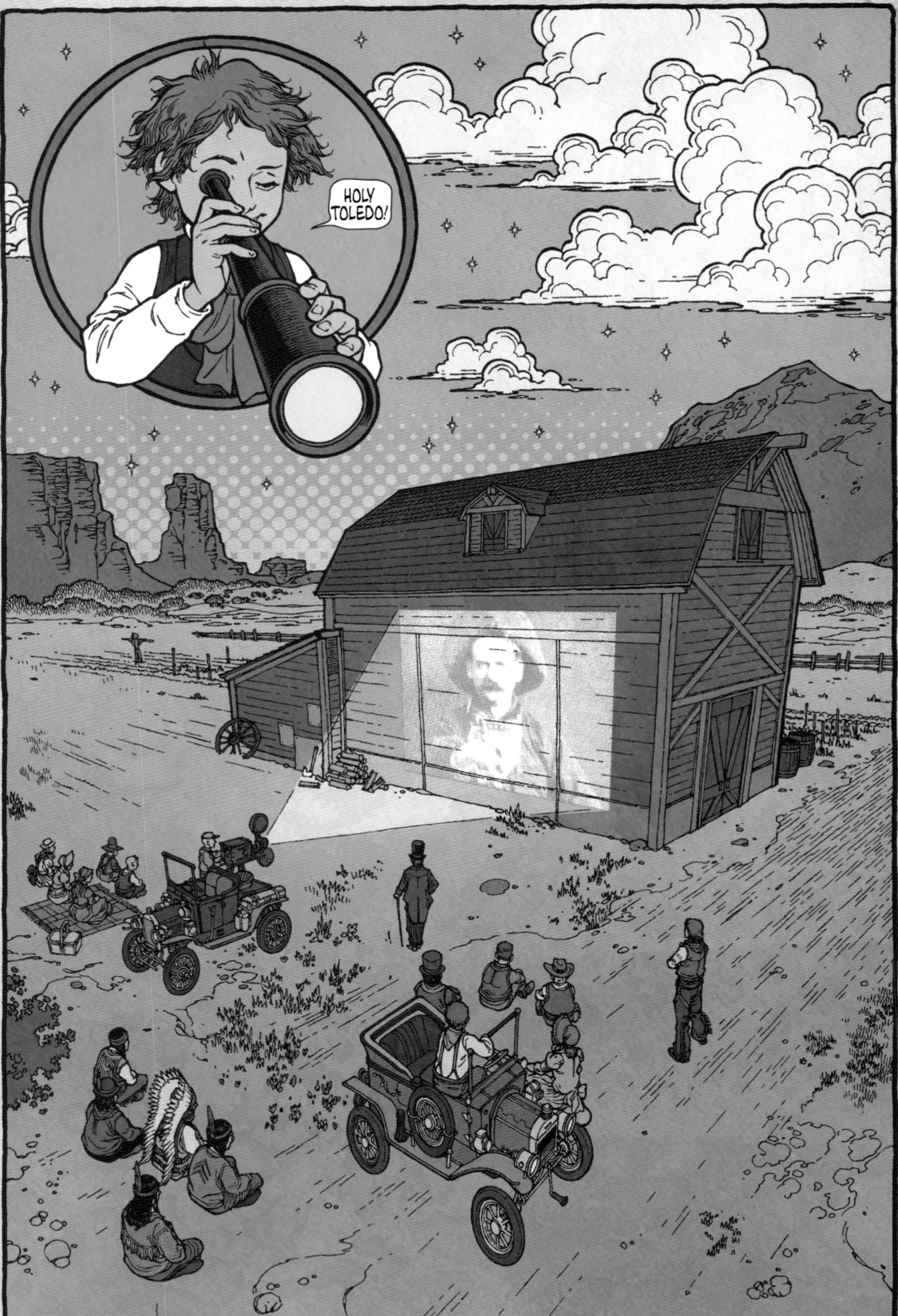
HOLY TOLEDO!
10

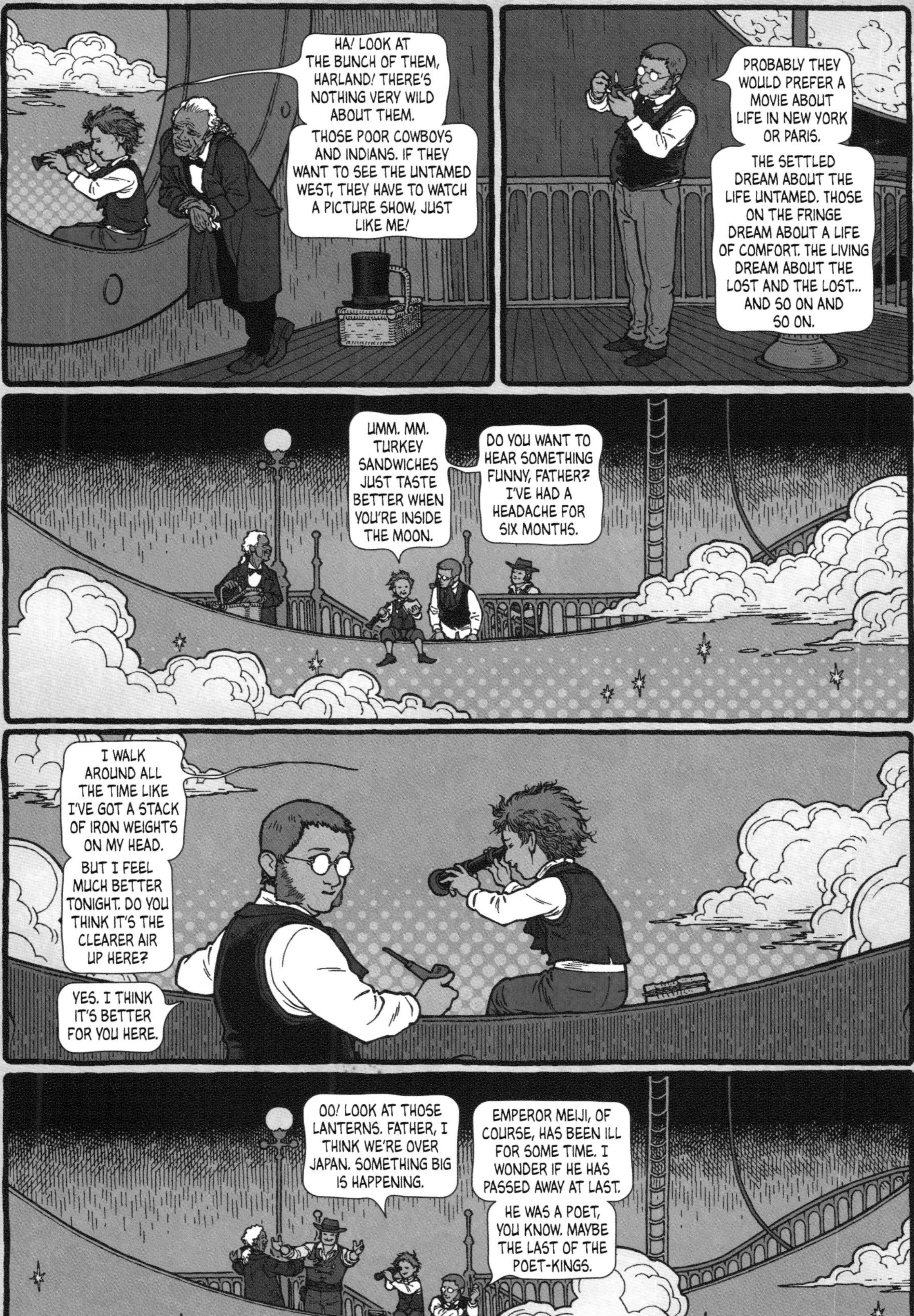
HA! LOOK AT THE BUNCH OF THEM, HARLAND! THERE'S NOTHING VERY WILD ABOUT THEM.
THOSE POOR COWBOYS AND INDIANS. IF THEY WANT TO SEE THE UNTAMED WEST, THEY HAVE TO WATCH A PICTURE SHOW, JUST LIKE ME!
PROBABLY THEY WOULD PREFER A MOVIE ABOUT LIFE IN NEW YORK OR PARIS.
THE SETTLED DREAM ABOUT THE LIFE UNTAMED. THOSE ON THE FRINGE DREAM ABOUT A LIFE OF COMFORT. THE LIVING DREAM ABOUT THE LOST AND THE LOST... AND SO ON AND SO ON.
UMM. MM. TURKEY SANDWICHES JUST TASTE BETTER WHEN YOU'RE INSIDE THE MOON.
DO YOU WANT TO HEAR SOMETHING FUNNY, FATHER? I'VE HAD A HEADACHE FOR SIX MONTHS.
I WALK AROUND ALL THE TIME LIKE I'VE GOT A STACK OF IRON WEIGHTS ON MY HEAD.
BUT I FEEL MUCH BETTER TONIGHT. DO YOU THINK IT'S THE CLEARER AIR UP HERE?
YES. I THINK IT'S BETTER FOR YOU HERE.
OO! LOOK AT THOSE LANTERNS. FATHER, I THINK WE'RE OVER JAPAN. SOMETHING BIG IS HAPPENING.
EMPEROR MEIJI, OF COURSE, HAS BEEN ILL FOR SOME TIME. I WONDER IF HE HAS PASSED AWAY AT LAST.
HE WAS A POET, YOU KNOW. MAYBE THE LAST OF THE POET-KINGS.
11

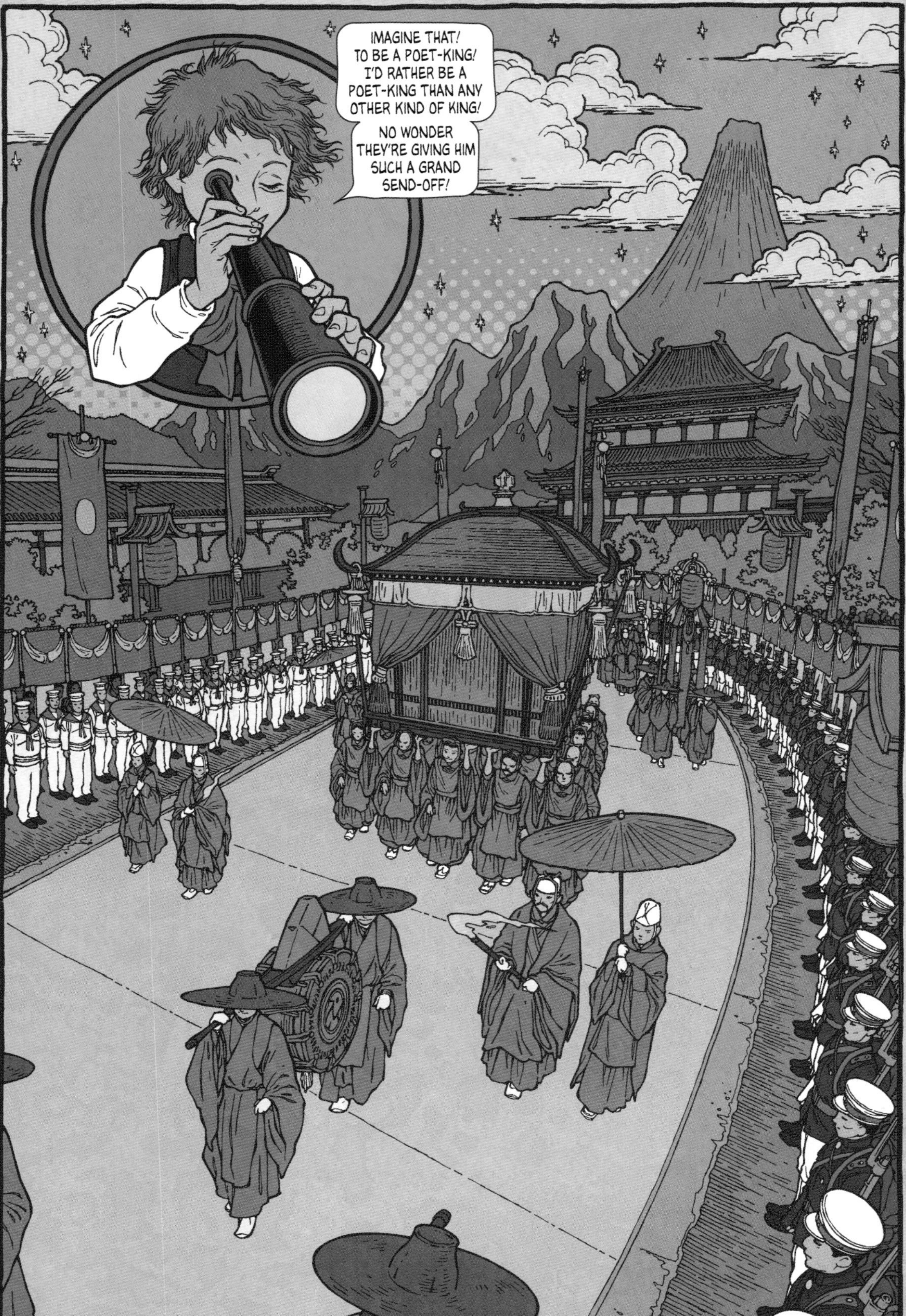
IMAGINE THAT! TO BE A POET-KING! I'D RATHER BE A POET-KING THAN ANY OTHER KIND OF KING!
NO WONDER THEY'RE GIVING HIM SUCH A GRAND SEND-OFF!
12

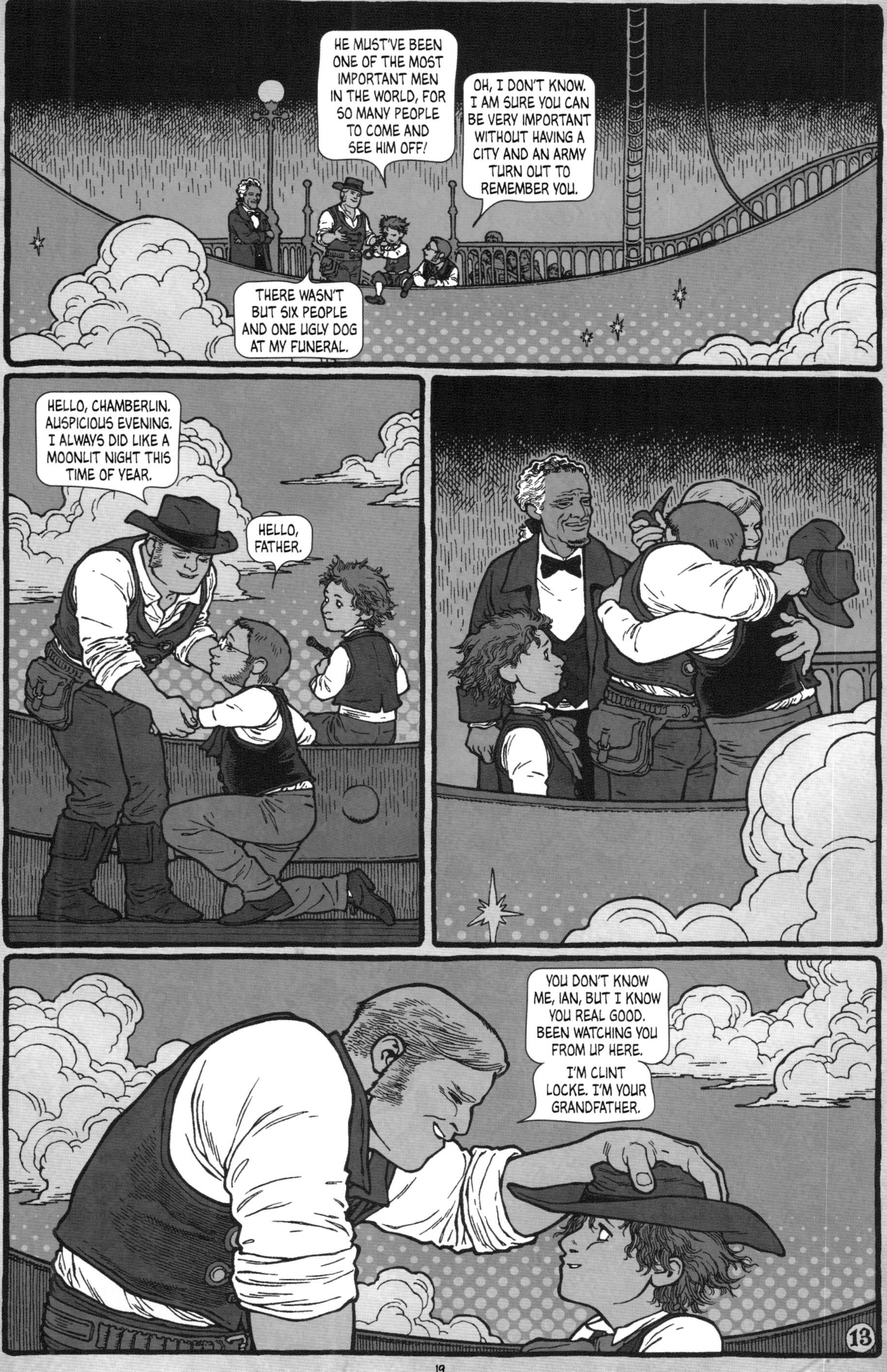
HE MUST'VE BEEN ONE OF THE MOST IMPORTANT MEN IN THE WORLD, FOR SO MANY PEOPLE TO COME AND SEE HIM OFF!
OH, I DON'T KNOW. I AM SURE YOU CAN BE VERY IMPORTANT WITHOUT HAVING A CITY AND AN ARMY TURN OUT TO REMEMBER YOU.
THERE WASN'T BUT SIX PEOPLE AND ONE UGLY DOG AT MY FUNERAL.
HELLO, CHAMBERLIN. AUSPICIOUS EVENING. I ALWAYS DID LIKE A MOONLIT NIGHT THIS TIME OF YEAR.
HELLO, FATHER.
YOU DON'T KNOW ME, IAN, BUT I KNOW YOU REAL GOOD. BEEN WATCHING YOU FROM UP HERE.
I'M CLINT LOCKE. I'M YOUR GRANDFATHER.
13

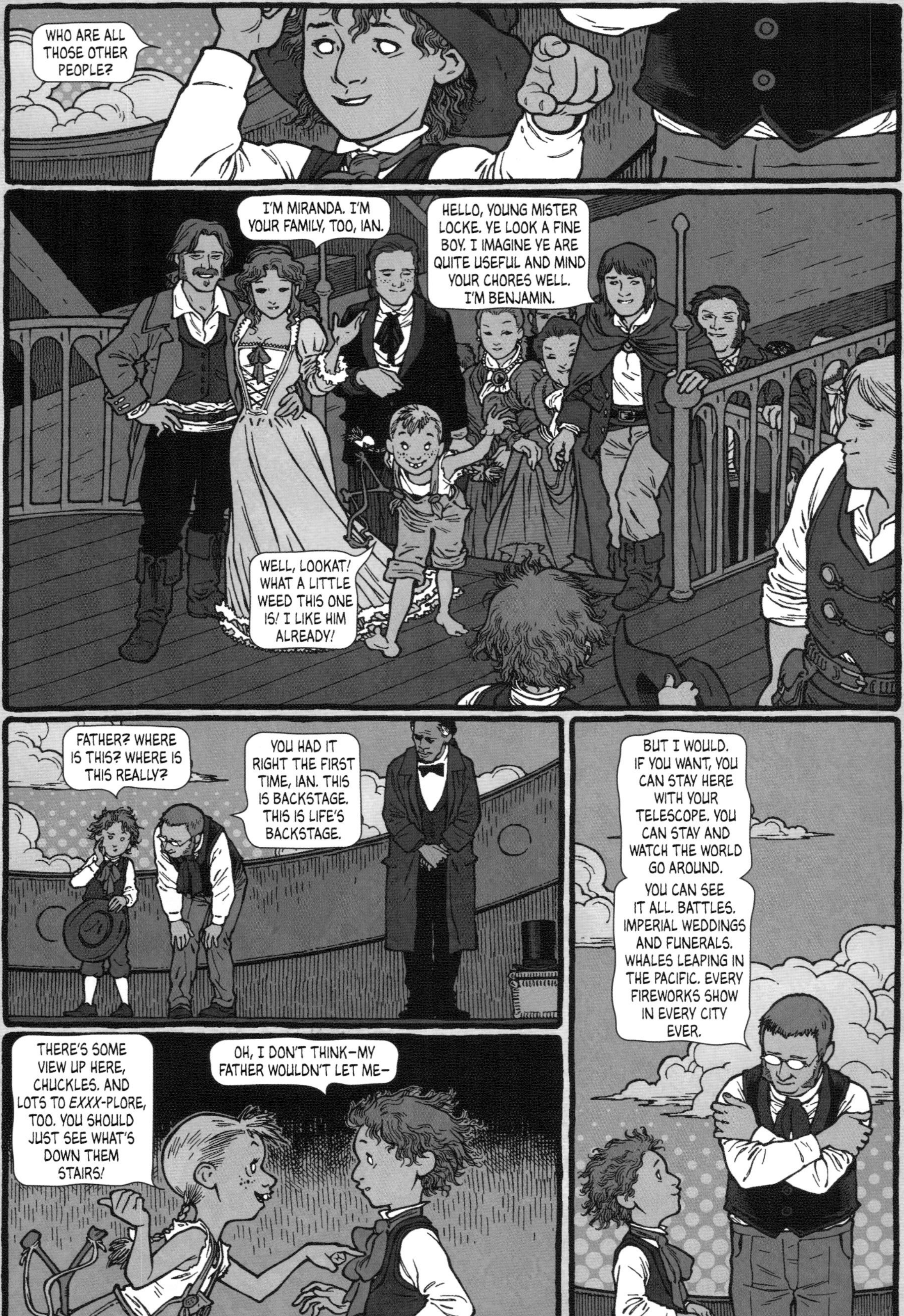
WHO ARE ALL THOSE OTHER PEOPLE?
I'M MIRANDA. I'M YOUR FAMILY, TOO, IAN.
HELLO, YOUNG MISTER LOCKE. YE LOOK A FINE BOY. I IMAGINE YE ARE QUITE USEFUL AND MIND YOUR CHORES WELL. I'M BENJAMIN.
WELL, LOOKAT! WHAT A LITTLE WEED THIS ONE IS! I LIKE HIM ALREADY!
FATHER? WHERE IS THIS? WHERE IS THIS REALLY?
YOU HAD IT RIGHT THE FIRST TIME, IAN. THIS IS BACKSTAGE. THIS IS LIFE'S BACKSTAGE.
BUT I WOULD. IF YOU WANT, YOU CAN STAY HERE WITH YOUR TELESCOPE. YOU CAN STAY AND WATCH THE WORLD GO AROUND.
YOU CAN SEE IT ALL. BATTLES. IMPERIAL WEDDINGS AND FUNERALS. WHALES LEAPING IN THE PACIFIC. EVERY FIREWORKS SHOW IN EVERY CITY EVER.
THERE'S SOME VIEW UP HERE, CHUCKLES. AND LOTS TO *EXXX*-PLORE, TOO. YOU SHOULD JUST SEE WHAT'S DOWN THEM STAIRS!
OH, I DON'T THINK—MY FATHER WOULDN'T LET ME—
14

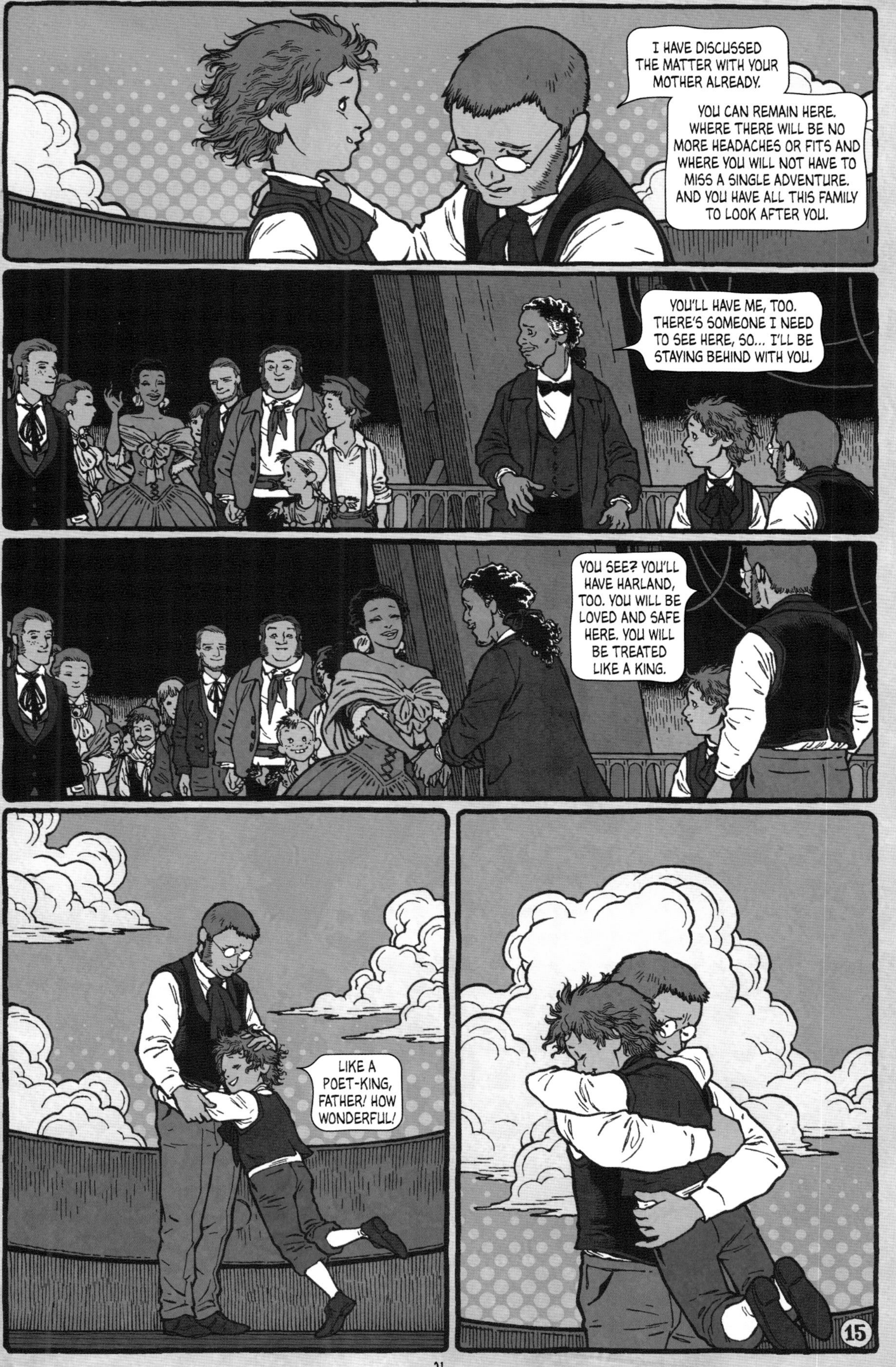
I HAVE DISCUSSED THE MATTER WITH YOUR MOTHER ALREADY.
YOU CAN REMAIN HERE. WHERE THERE WILL BE NO MORE HEADACHES OR FITS AND WHERE YOU WILL NOT HAVE TO MISS A SINGLE ADVENTURE. AND YOU HAVE ALL THIS FAMILY TO LOOK AFTER YOU.
YOU'LL HAVE ME, TOO. THERE'S SOMEONE I NEED TO SEE HERE, SO... I'LL BE STAYING BEHIND WITH YOU.
YOU SEE? YOU'LL HAVE HARLAND, TOO. YOU WILL BE LOVED AND SAFE HERE. YOU WILL BE TREATED LIKE A KING.
LIKE A POET-KING, FATHER! HOW WONDERFUL!
15

I GOT HIM. I'LL LOOK AFTER HIM.

I'M NOT WORRIED. I KNOW NOTHING BAD WILL HAPPEN... HERE.

SEE YOU AGAIN SOON, FATHER!

YES. BEFORE YOU KNOW IT.

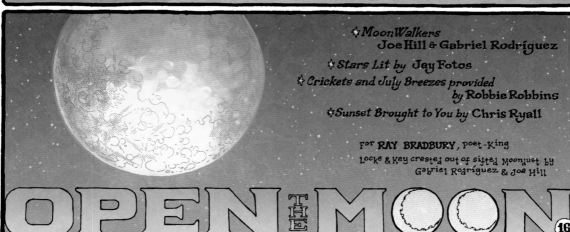

✧ MoonWalkers
  Joe Hill & Gabriel Rodríguez
✧ Stars Lit by Jay Fotos
✧ Crickets and July Breezes provided
  by Robbie Robbins
✧ Sunset Brought to You by Chris Ryall

FOR RAY BRADBURY, Poet-King
Locke & Key created out of sifted Moondust by
Gabriel Rodríguez & Joe Hill

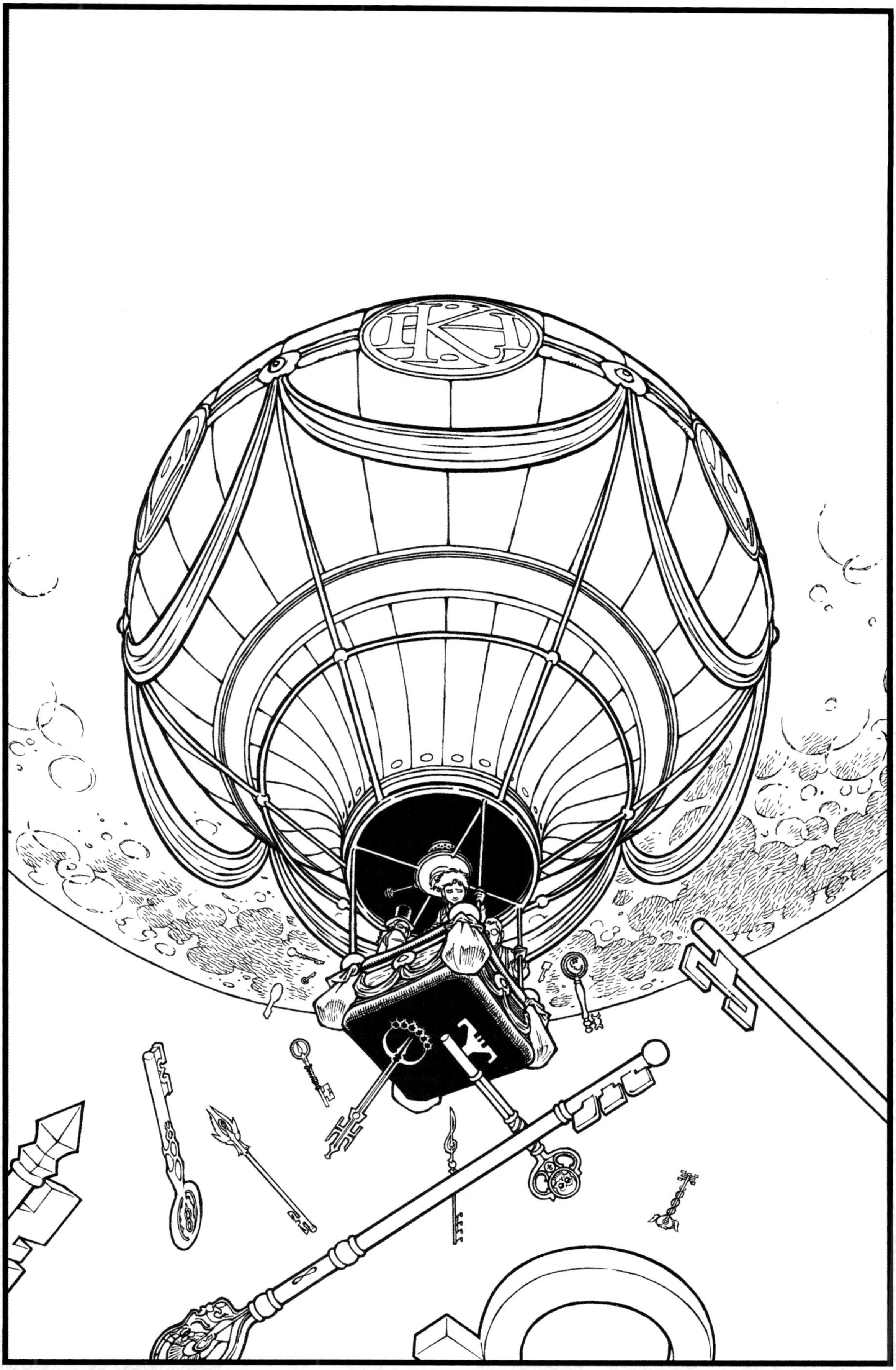

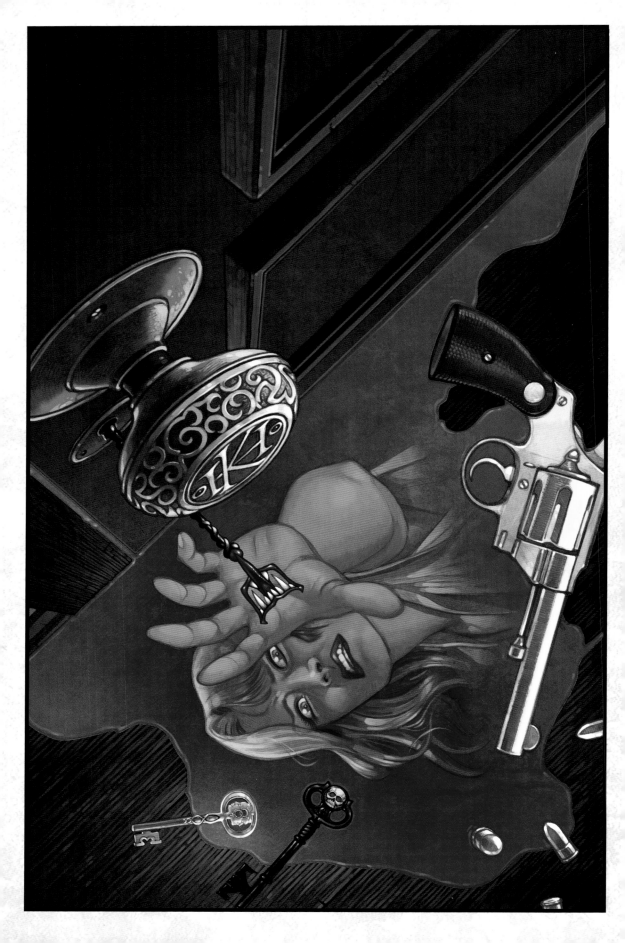

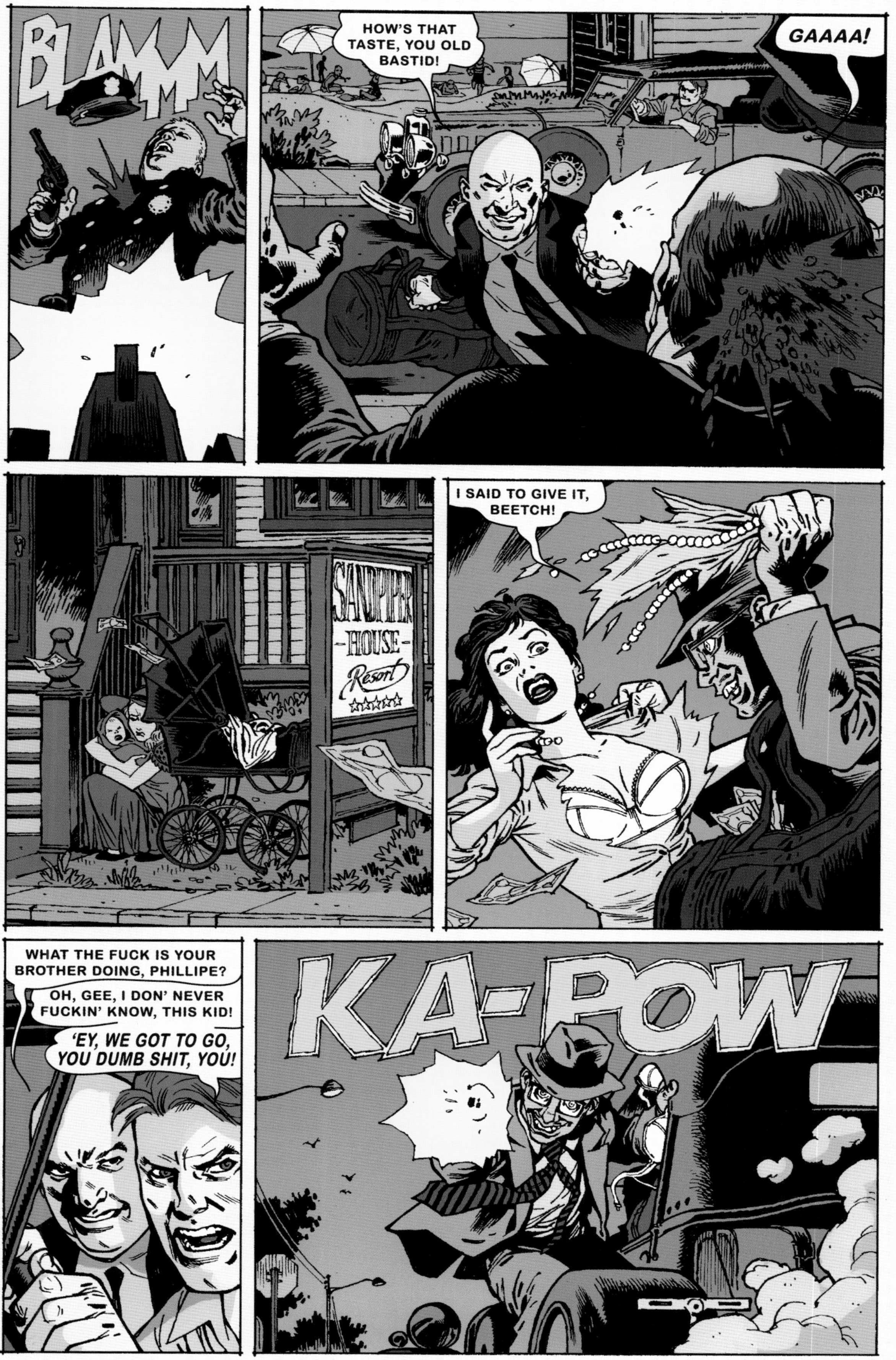
BLAMMM
HOW'S THAT TASTE, YOU OLD BASTID!
GAAAA!
SANDPIPER HOUSE Resort
I SAID TO GIVE IT, BEETCH!
WHAT THE FUCK IS YOUR BROTHER DOING, PHILLIPE?
OH, GEE, I DON' NEVER FUCKIN' KNOW, THIS KID!
'EY, WE GOT TO GO, YOU DUMB SHIT, YOU!
KA-POW

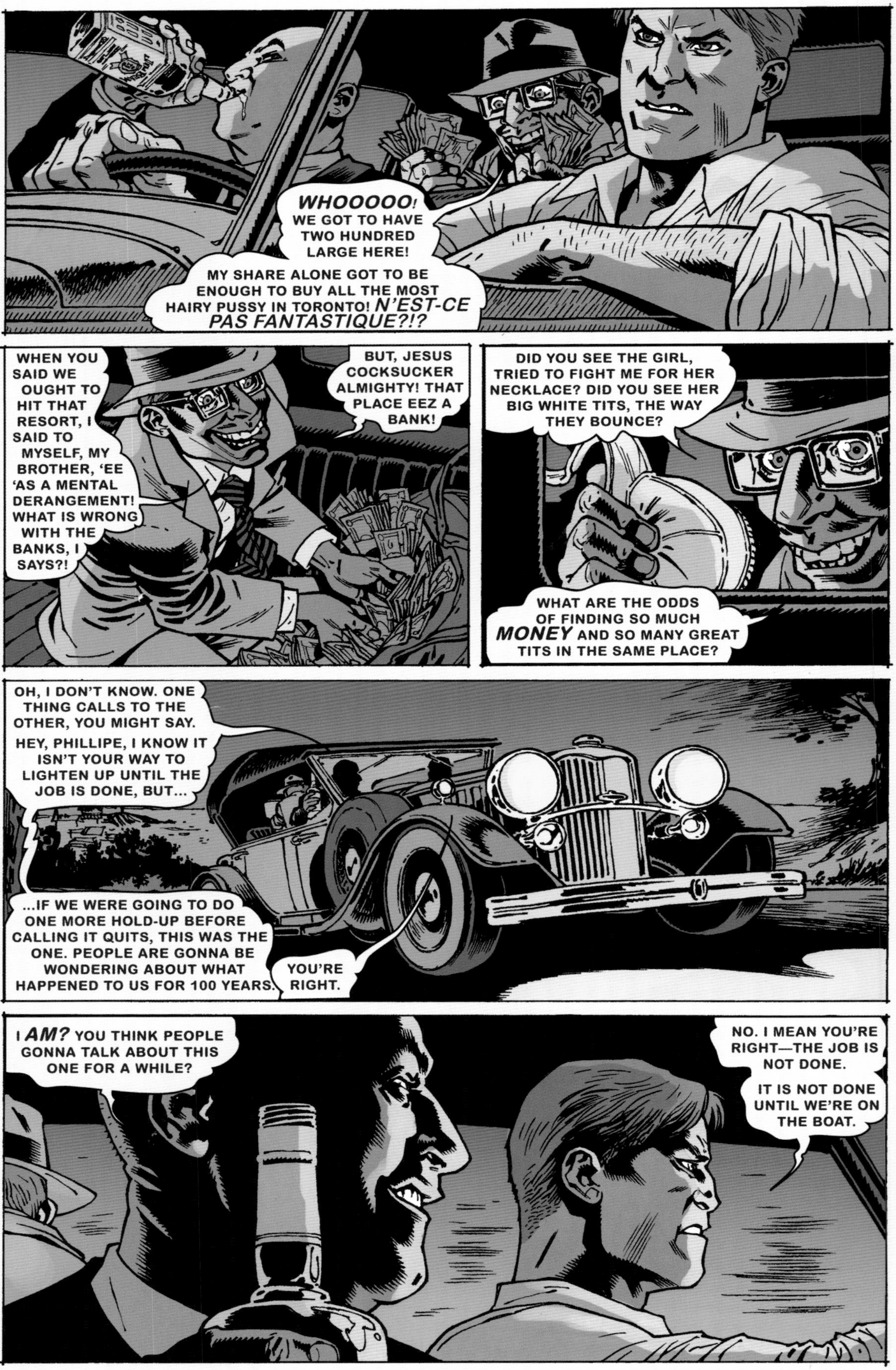
WHOOOOO! WE GOT TO HAVE TWO HUNDRED LARGE HERE!
MY SHARE ALONE GOT TO BE ENOUGH TO BUY ALL THE MOST HAIRY PUSSY IN TORONTO! N'EST-CE PAS FANTASTIQUE?!?
WHEN YOU SAID WE OUGHT TO HIT THAT RESORT, I SAID TO MYSELF, MY BROTHER, 'EE 'AS A MENTAL DERANGEMENT! WHAT IS WRONG WITH THE BANKS, I SAYS?!
BUT, JESUS COCKSUCKER ALMIGHTY! THAT PLACE EEZ A BANK!
DID YOU SEE THE GIRL, TRIED TO FIGHT ME FOR HER NECKLACE? DID YOU SEE HER BIG WHITE TITS, THE WAY THEY BOUNCE?
WHAT ARE THE ODDS OF FINDING SO MUCH MONEY AND SO MANY GREAT TITS IN THE SAME PLACE?
OH, I DON'T KNOW. ONE THING CALLS TO THE OTHER, YOU MIGHT SAY.
HEY, PHILLIPE, I KNOW IT ISN'T YOUR WAY TO LIGHTEN UP UNTIL THE JOB IS DONE, BUT...
...IF WE WERE GOING TO DO ONE MORE HOLD-UP BEFORE CALLING IT QUITS, THIS WAS THE ONE. PEOPLE ARE GONNA BE WONDERING ABOUT WHAT HAPPENED TO US FOR 100 YEARS.
YOU'RE RIGHT.
I AM? YOU THINK PEOPLE GONNA TALK ABOUT THIS ONE FOR A WHILE?
NO. I MEAN YOU'RE RIGHT—THE JOB IS NOT DONE.
IT IS NOT DONE UNTIL WE'RE ON THE BOAT.

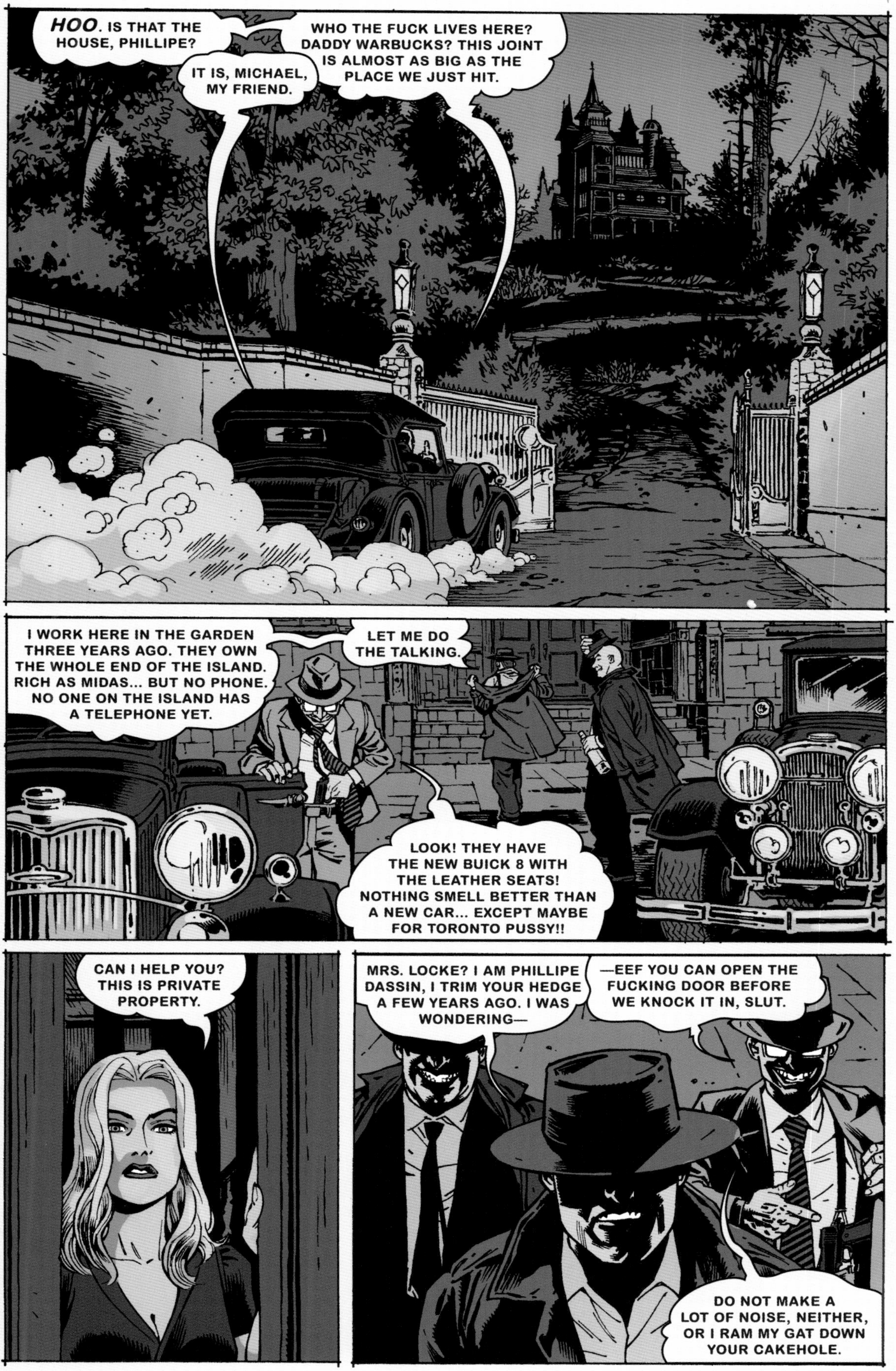
HOO. IS THAT THE HOUSE, PHILLIPE?
IT IS, MICHAEL, MY FRIEND.
WHO THE FUCK LIVES HERE? DADDY WARBUCKS? THIS JOINT IS ALMOST AS BIG AS THE PLACE WE JUST HIT.
I WORK HERE IN THE GARDEN THREE YEARS AGO. THEY OWN THE WHOLE END OF THE ISLAND. RICH AS MIDAS... BUT NO PHONE. NO ONE ON THE ISLAND HAS A TELEPHONE YET.
LET ME DO THE TALKING.
LOOK! THEY HAVE THE NEW BUICK 8 WITH THE LEATHER SEATS! NOTHING SMELL BETTER THAN A NEW CAR... EXCEPT MAYBE FOR TORONTO PUSSY!!
CAN I HELP YOU? THIS IS PRIVATE PROPERTY.
MRS. LOCKE? I AM PHILLIPE DASSIN, I TRIM YOUR HEDGE A FEW YEARS AGO. I WAS WONDERING—
—EEF YOU CAN OPEN THE FUCKING DOOR BEFORE WE KNOCK IT IN, SLUT.
DO NOT MAKE A LOT OF NOISE, NEITHER, OR I RAM MY GAT DOWN YOUR CAKEHOLE.

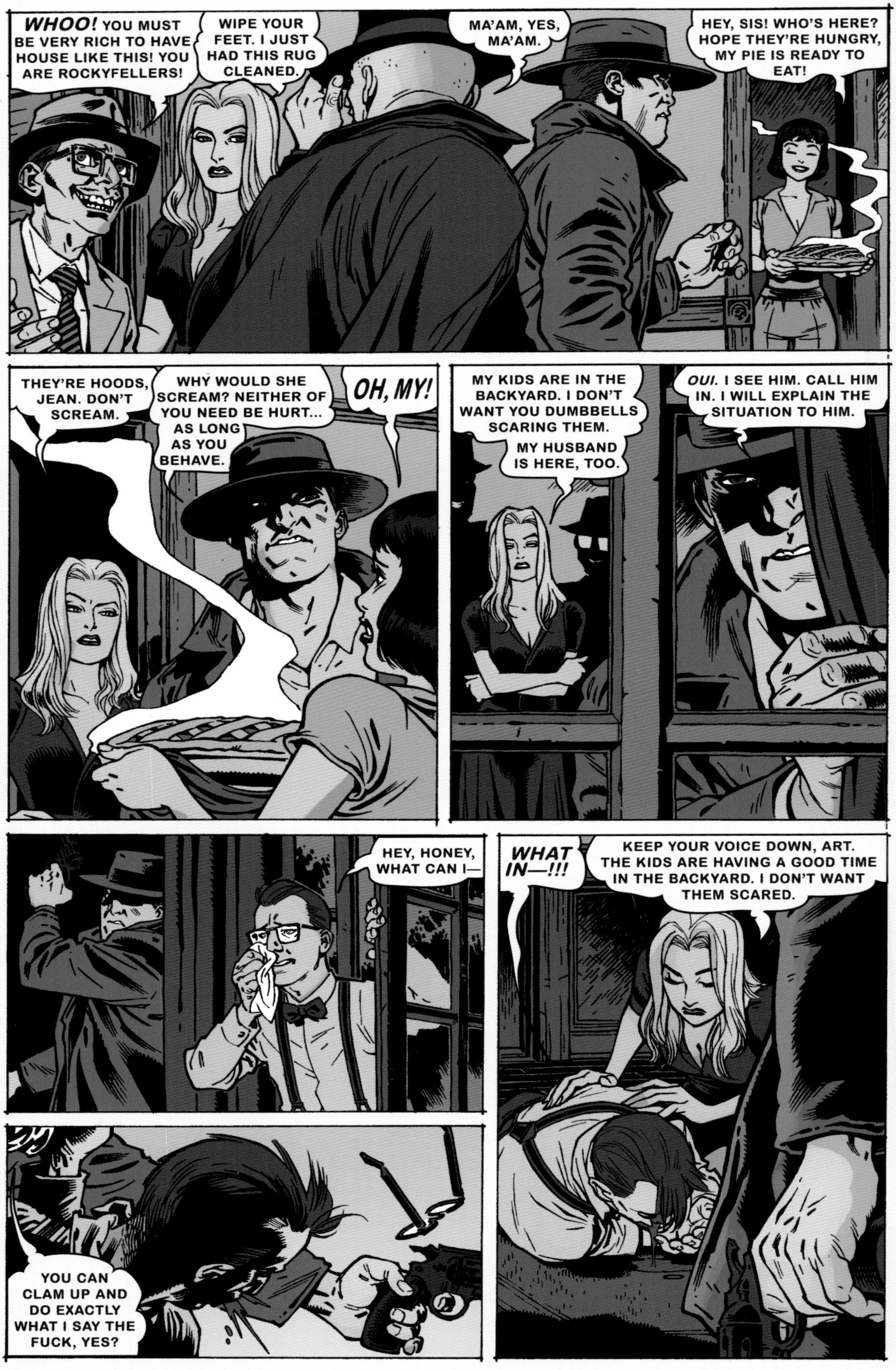
WHOO! YOU MUST BE VERY RICH TO HAVE HOUSE LIKE THIS! YOU ARE ROCKYFELLERS!
WIPE YOUR FEET. I JUST HAD THIS RUG CLEANED.
MA'AM, YES, MA'AM.
HEY, SIS! WHO'S HERE? HOPE THEY'RE HUNGRY, MY PIE IS READY TO EAT!
THEY'RE HOODS, JEAN. DON'T SCREAM.
WHY WOULD SHE SCREAM? NEITHER OF YOU NEED BE HURT... AS LONG AS YOU BEHAVE.
OH, MY!
MY KIDS ARE IN THE BACKYARD. I DON'T WANT YOU DUMBBELLS SCARING THEM.
MY HUSBAND IS HERE, TOO.
OUI. I SEE HIM. CALL HIM IN. I WILL EXPLAIN THE SITUATION TO HIM.
HEY, HONEY, WHAT CAN I—
YOU CAN CLAM UP AND DO EXACTLY WHAT I SAY THE FUCK, YES?
WHAT IN—!!!
KEEP YOUR VOICE DOWN, ART. THE KIDS ARE HAVING A GOOD TIME IN THE BACKYARD. I DON'T WANT THEM SCARED.

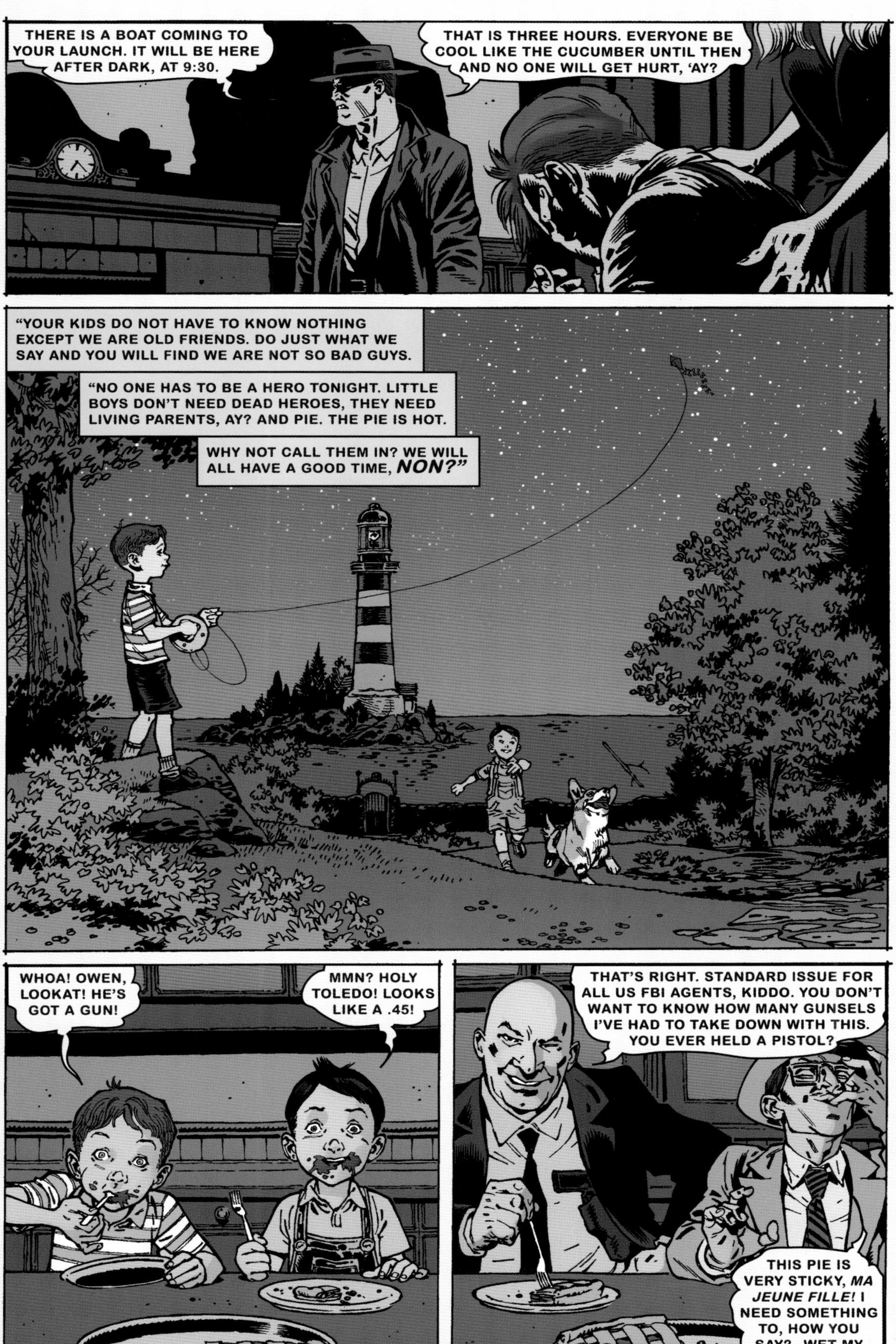
THERE IS A BOAT COMING TO YOUR LAUNCH. IT WILL BE HERE AFTER DARK, AT 9:30.
THAT IS THREE HOURS. EVERYONE BE COOL LIKE THE CUCUMBER UNTIL THEN AND NO ONE WILL GET HURT, 'AY?
"YOUR KIDS DO NOT HAVE TO KNOW NOTHING EXCEPT WE ARE OLD FRIENDS. DO JUST WHAT WE SAY AND YOU WILL FIND WE ARE NOT SO BAD GUYS.
"NO ONE HAS TO BE A HERO TONIGHT. LITTLE BOYS DON'T NEED DEAD HEROES, THEY NEED LIVING PARENTS, AY? AND PIE. THE PIE IS HOT.
WHY NOT CALL THEM IN? WE WILL ALL HAVE A GOOD TIME, ***NON?"***
WHOA! OWEN, LOOKAT! HE'S GOT A GUN!
MMN? HOLY TOLEDO! LOOKS LIKE A .45!
THAT'S RIGHT. STANDARD ISSUE FOR ALL US FBI AGENTS, KIDDO. YOU DON'T WANT TO KNOW HOW MANY GUNSELS I'VE HAD TO TAKE DOWN WITH THIS. YOU EVER HELD A PISTOL?
THIS PIE IS VERY STICKY, *MA JEUNE FILLE!* I NEED SOMETHING TO, HOW YOU SAY?—WET MY WHISTLE!

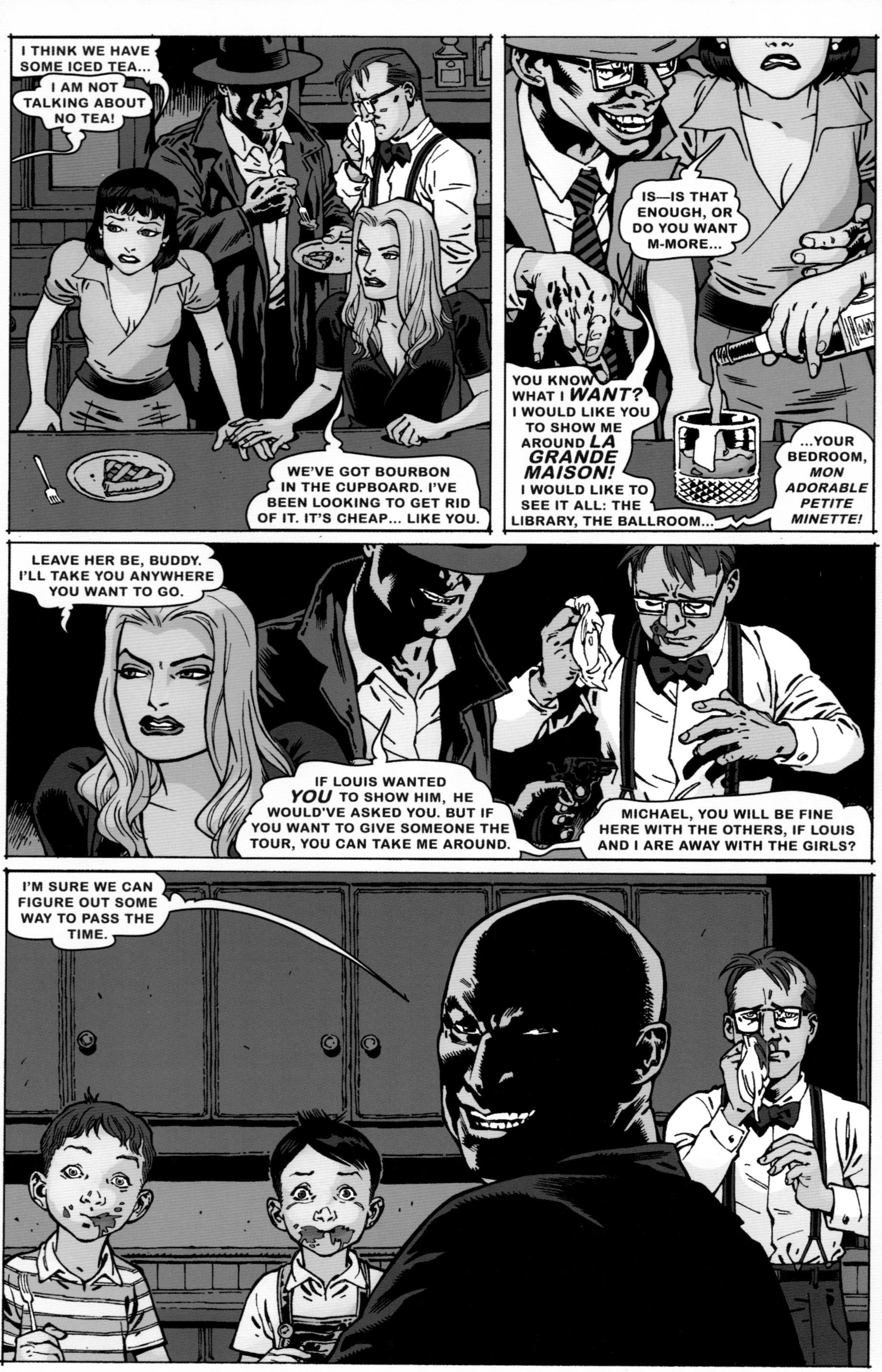

I THINK WE HAVE SOME ICED TEA...
I AM NOT TALKING ABOUT NO TEA!
WE'VE GOT BOURBON IN THE CUPBOARD. I'VE BEEN LOOKING TO GET RID OF IT. IT'S CHEAP... LIKE YOU.
IS—IS THAT ENOUGH, OR DO YOU WANT M-MORE...
YOU KNOW WHAT I WANT? I WOULD LIKE YOU TO SHOW ME AROUND LA GRANDE MAISON! I WOULD LIKE TO SEE IT ALL: THE LIBRARY, THE BALLROOM...
...YOUR BEDROOM, MON ADORABLE PETITE MINETTE!
LEAVE HER BE, BUDDY. I'LL TAKE YOU ANYWHERE YOU WANT TO GO.
IF LOUIS WANTED YOU TO SHOW HIM, HE WOULD'VE ASKED YOU. BUT IF YOU WANT TO GIVE SOMEONE THE TOUR, YOU CAN TAKE ME AROUND.
MICHAEL, YOU WILL BE FINE HERE WITH THE OTHERS, IF LOUIS AND I ARE AWAY WITH THE GIRLS?
I'M SURE WE CAN FIGURE OUT SOME WAY TO PASS THE TIME.

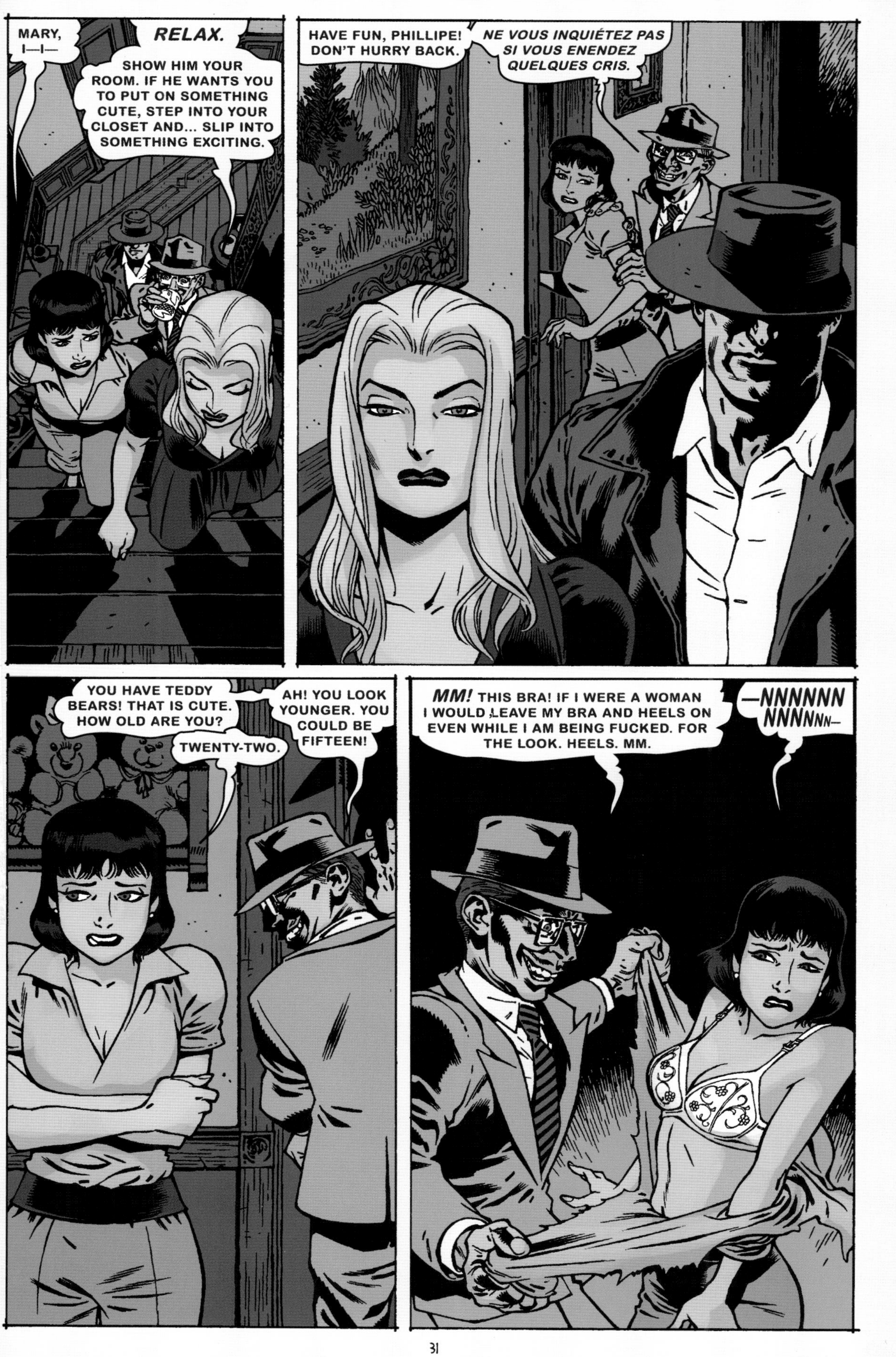
MARY, I—I—
RELAX.
SHOW HIM YOUR ROOM. IF HE WANTS YOU TO PUT ON SOMETHING CUTE, STEP INTO YOUR CLOSET AND... SLIP INTO SOMETHING EXCITING.
HAVE FUN, PHILLIPE! DON'T HURRY BACK.
NE VOUS INQUIÉTEZ PAS SI VOUS ENENDEZ QUELQUES CRIS.
YOU HAVE TEDDY BEARS! THAT IS CUTE. HOW OLD ARE YOU?
TWENTY-TWO.
AH! YOU LOOK YOUNGER. YOU COULD BE FIFTEEN!
MM! THIS BRA! IF I WERE A WOMAN I WOULD LEAVE MY BRA AND HEELS ON EVEN WHILE I AM BEING FUCKED. FOR THE LOOK. HEELS. MM.
—NNNNNN NNNNnn—

SO WHAT DO YOU WANT? MONEY... OR ME?

MAYBE BOTH.

WE CAN START WITH YOUR JEWELS, THOUGH. YOUR MONEY. ANY VALUABLES YOU MIGHT HAVE.

BE A HON AND GIVE ME ONE OF THOSE COFFIN NAILS. I COULD USE SOMETHING TO SETTLE MY NERVES.

YOUR NERVES SEEM PRETTY OKAY TO ME.

I FAKE IT WELL. BELIEVE ME, I'M NOT REAL RELAXED ABOUT THE IDEA THAT YOUR BROTHER IS RAPING MY SISTER.

MAYBE YOUR SISTER WILL LIKE IT. SHE SEEMS UPTIGHT. MAYBE SHE NEEDS A GOOD FUCK TO LOOSEN HER UP.

THAT'S WHAT *YOU* THINK, BUD. BUT YOU CAN'T TAKE THE VALUABLES... IF YOU DON'T KNOW WHAT THEY *ARE.*

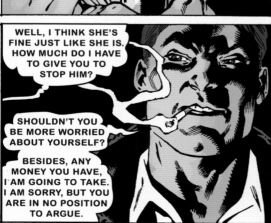

WELL, I THINK SHE'S FINE JUST LIKE SHE IS. HOW MUCH DO I HAVE TO GIVE YOU TO STOP HIM?

SHOULDN'T YOU BE MORE WORRIED ABOUT YOURSELF?

BESIDES, ANY MONEY YOU HAVE, I AM GOING TO TAKE. I AM SORRY, BUT YOU ARE IN NO POSITION TO ARGUE.

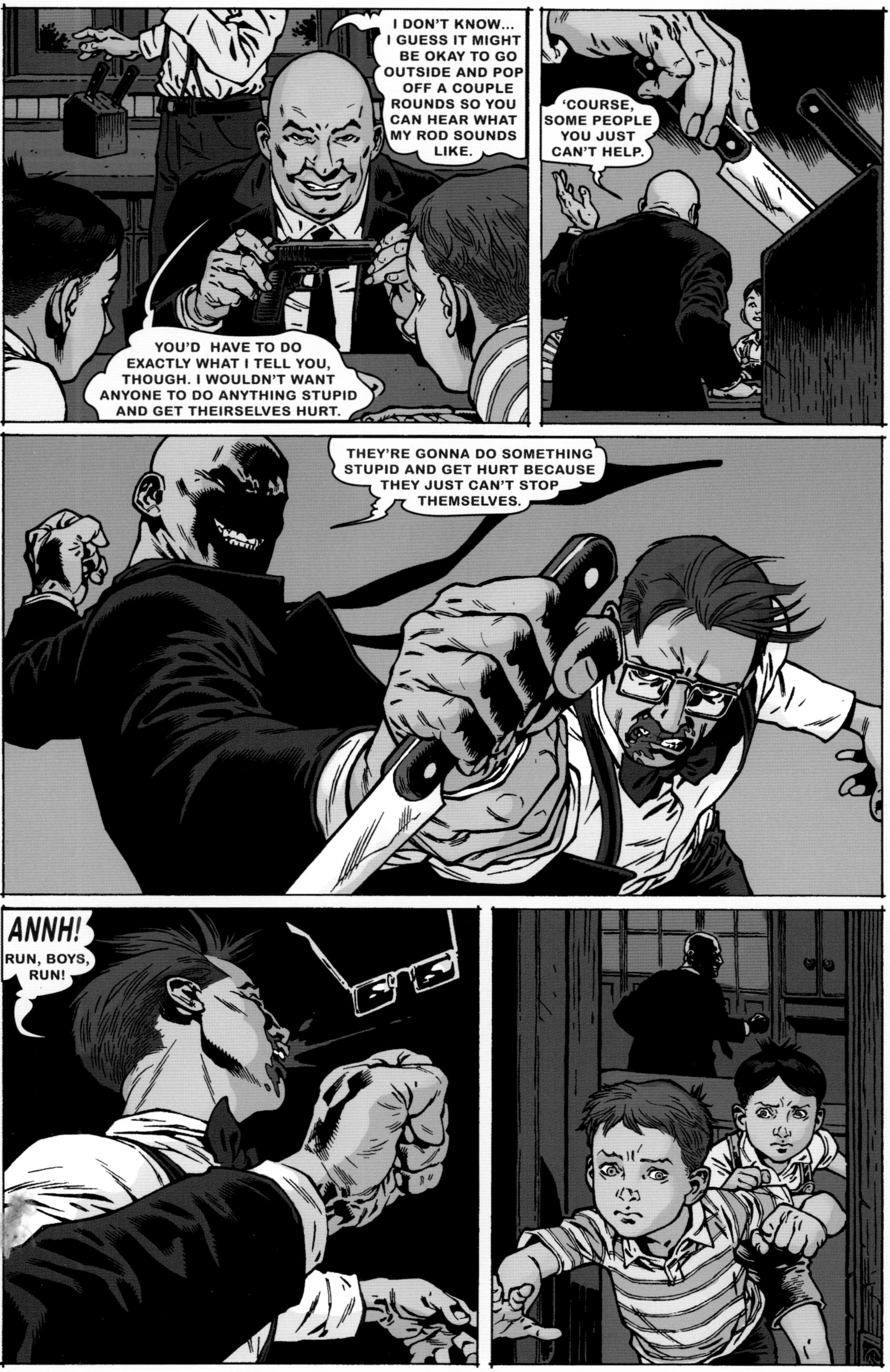

I DON'T KNOW... I GUESS IT MIGHT BE OKAY TO GO OUTSIDE AND POP OFF A COUPLE ROUNDS SO YOU CAN HEAR WHAT MY ROD SOUNDS LIKE.
YOU'D HAVE TO DO EXACTLY WHAT I TELL YOU, THOUGH. I WOULDN'T WANT ANYONE TO DO ANYTHING STUPID AND GET THEIRSELVES HURT.
'COURSE, SOME PEOPLE YOU JUST CAN'T HELP.
THEY'RE GONNA DO SOMETHING STUPID AND GET HURT BECAUSE THEY JUST CAN'T STOP THEMSELVES.
ANNH!
RUN, BOYS, RUN!

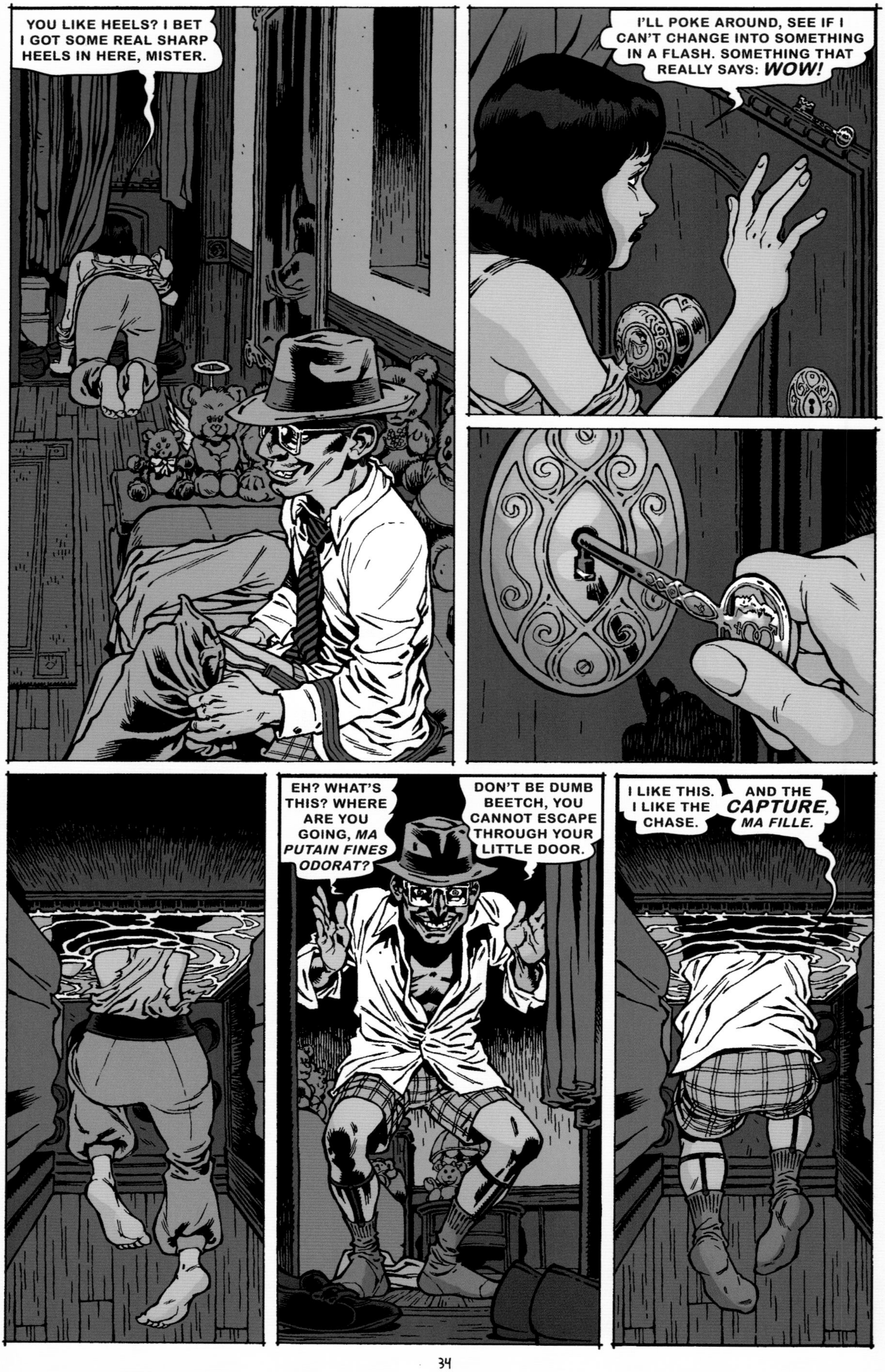
YOU LIKE HEELS? I BET I GOT SOME REAL SHARP HEELS IN HERE, MISTER.
I'LL POKE AROUND, SEE IF I CAN'T CHANGE INTO SOMETHING IN A FLASH. SOMETHING THAT REALLY SAYS: *WOW!*
EH? WHAT'S THIS? WHERE ARE YOU GOING, *MA PUTAIN FINES ODORAT?*
DON'T BE DUMB BEETCH, YOU CANNOT ESCAPE THROUGH YOUR LITTLE DOOR.
I LIKE THIS. I LIKE THE CHASE.
AND THE *CAPTURE*, *MA FILLE.*

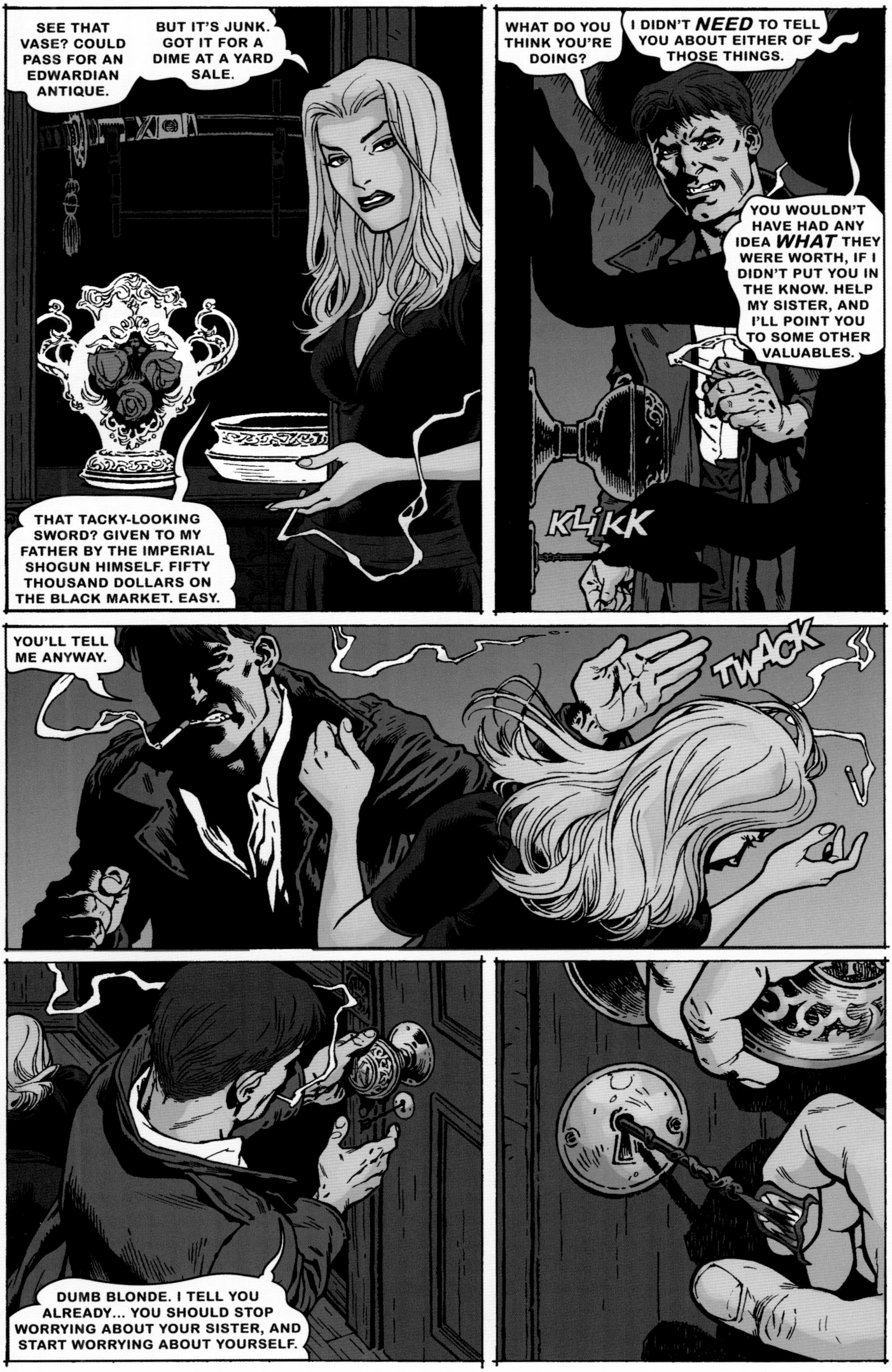
SEE THAT VASE? COULD PASS FOR AN EDWARDIAN ANTIQUE.
BUT IT'S JUNK. GOT IT FOR A DIME AT A YARD SALE.
THAT TACKY-LOOKING SWORD? GIVEN TO MY FATHER BY THE IMPERIAL SHOGUN HIMSELF. FIFTY THOUSAND DOLLARS ON THE BLACK MARKET. EASY.
WHAT DO YOU THINK YOU'RE DOING?
I DIDN'T NEED TO TELL YOU ABOUT EITHER OF THOSE THINGS.
YOU WOULDN'T HAVE HAD ANY IDEA WHAT THEY WERE WORTH, IF I DIDN'T PUT YOU IN THE KNOW. HELP MY SISTER, AND I'LL POINT YOU TO SOME OTHER VALUABLES.
KLIKK
YOU'LL TELL ME ANYWAY.
TWACK
DUMB BLONDE. I TELL YOU ALREADY... YOU SHOULD STOP WORRYING ABOUT YOUR SISTER, AND START WORRYING ABOUT YOURSELF.

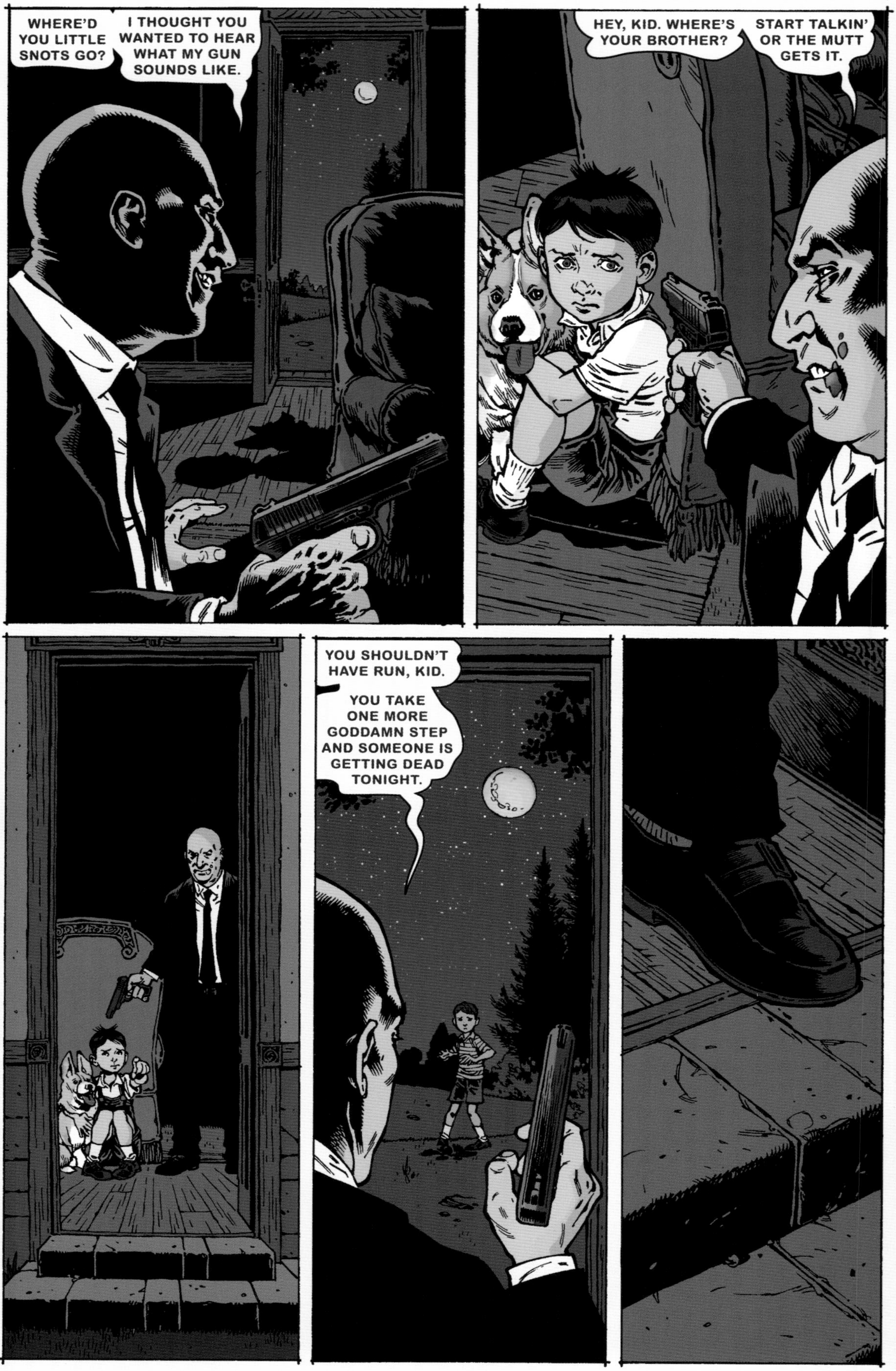
WHERE'D YOU LITTLE SNOTS GO?
I THOUGHT YOU WANTED TO HEAR WHAT MY GUN SOUNDS LIKE.
HEY, KID. WHERE'S YOUR BROTHER?
START TALKIN' OR THE MUTT GETS IT.
YOU SHOULDN'T HAVE RUN, KID.
YOU TAKE ONE MORE GODDAMN STEP AND SOMEONE IS GETTING DEAD TONIGHT.

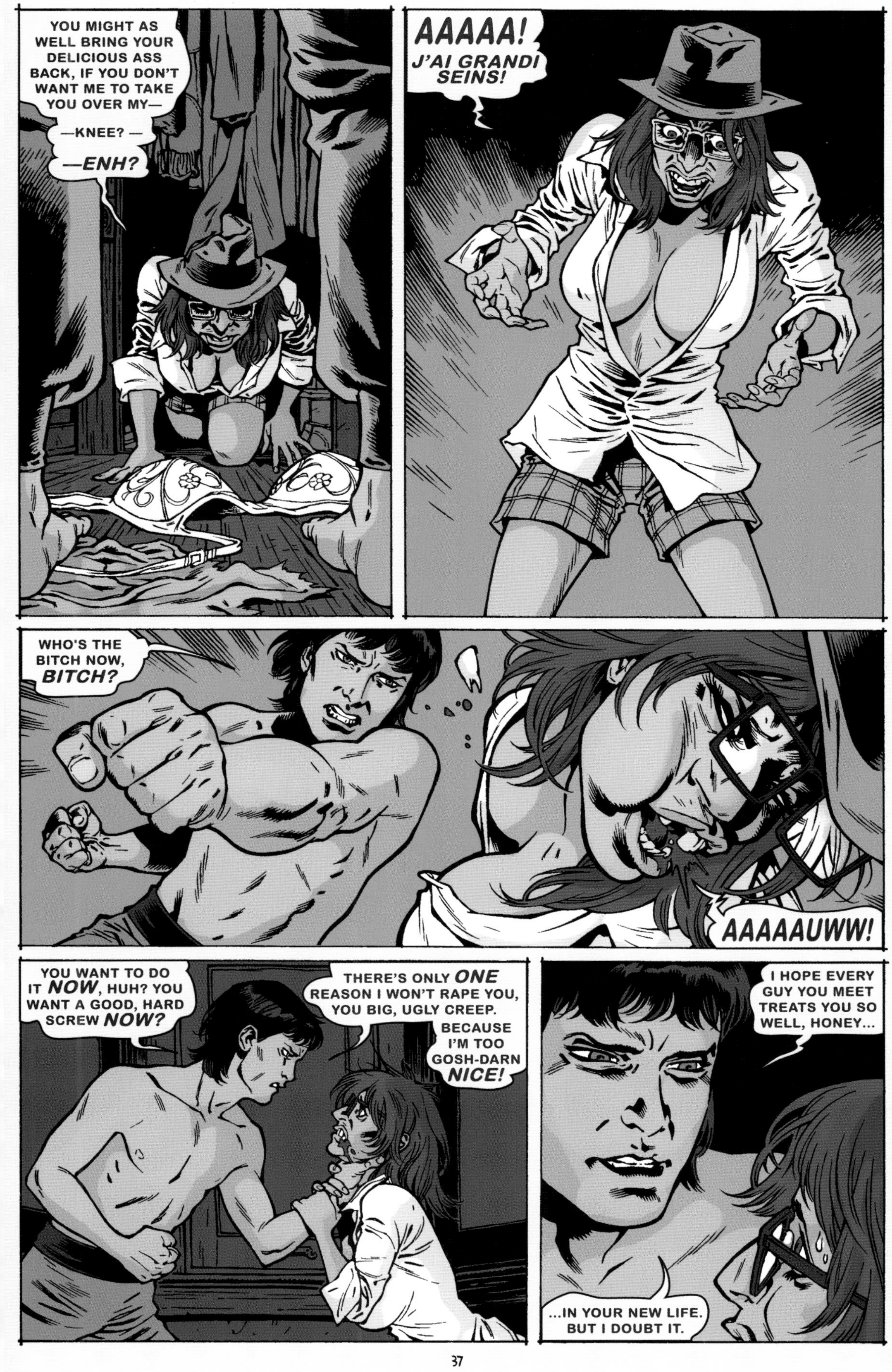
YOU MIGHT AS WELL BRING YOUR DELICIOUS ASS BACK, IF YOU DON'T WANT ME TO TAKE YOU OVER MY—
—KNEE? —
—ENH?
AAAAA! J'AI GRANDI SEINS!
WHO'S THE BITCH NOW, BITCH?
AAAAAUWW!
YOU WANT TO DO IT NOW, HUH? YOU WANT A GOOD, HARD SCREW NOW?
THERE'S ONLY ONE REASON I WON'T RAPE YOU, YOU BIG, UGLY CREEP.
BECAUSE I'M TOO GOSH-DARN NICE!
I HOPE EVERY GUY YOU MEET TREATS YOU SO WELL, HONEY...
...IN YOUR NEW LIFE. BUT I DOUBT IT.

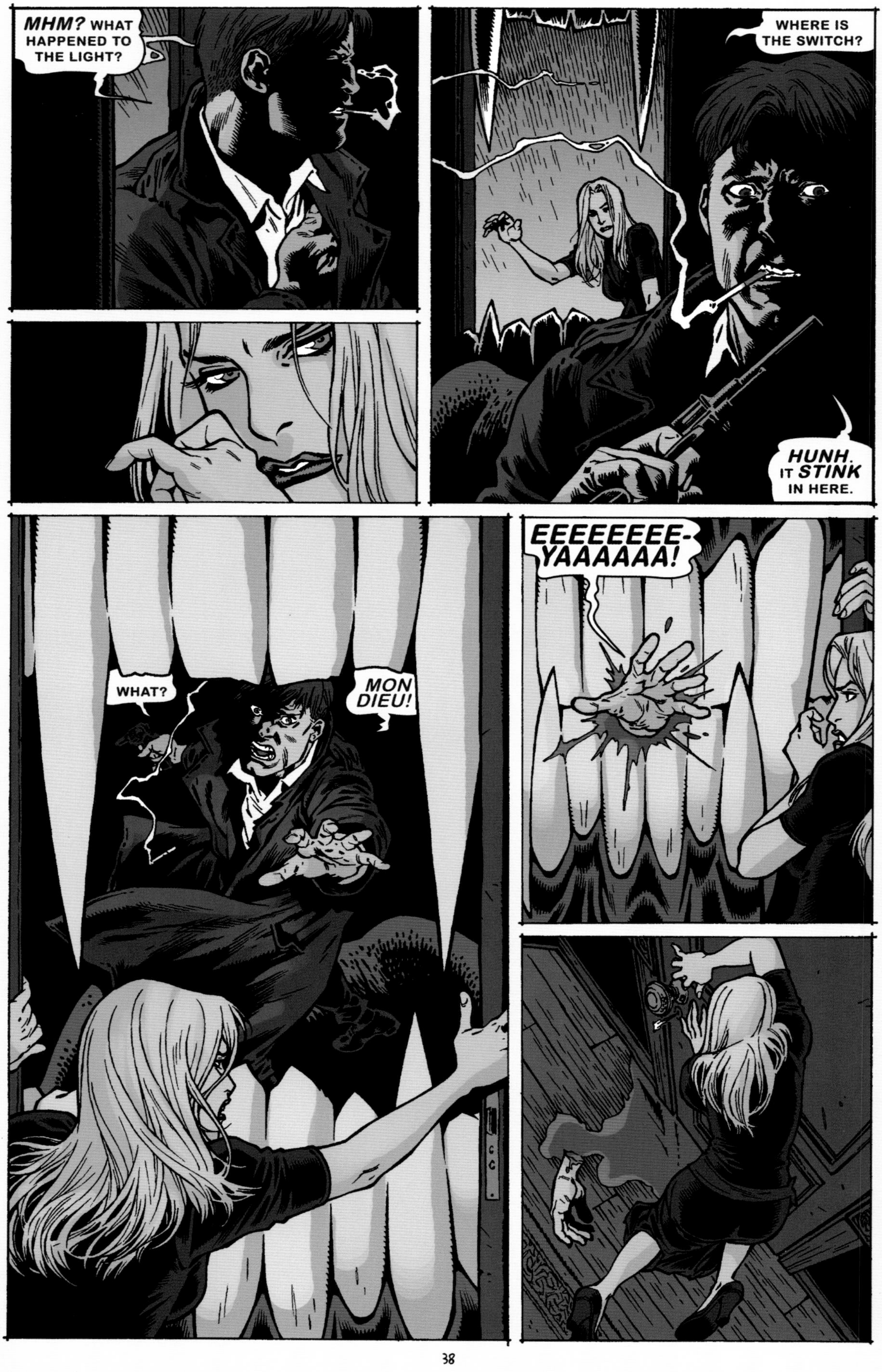
MHM? WHAT HAPPENED TO THE LIGHT?
WHERE IS THE SWITCH?
HUNH. IT STINK IN HERE.
WHAT?
MON DIEU!
EEEEEEEE-YAAAAAA!

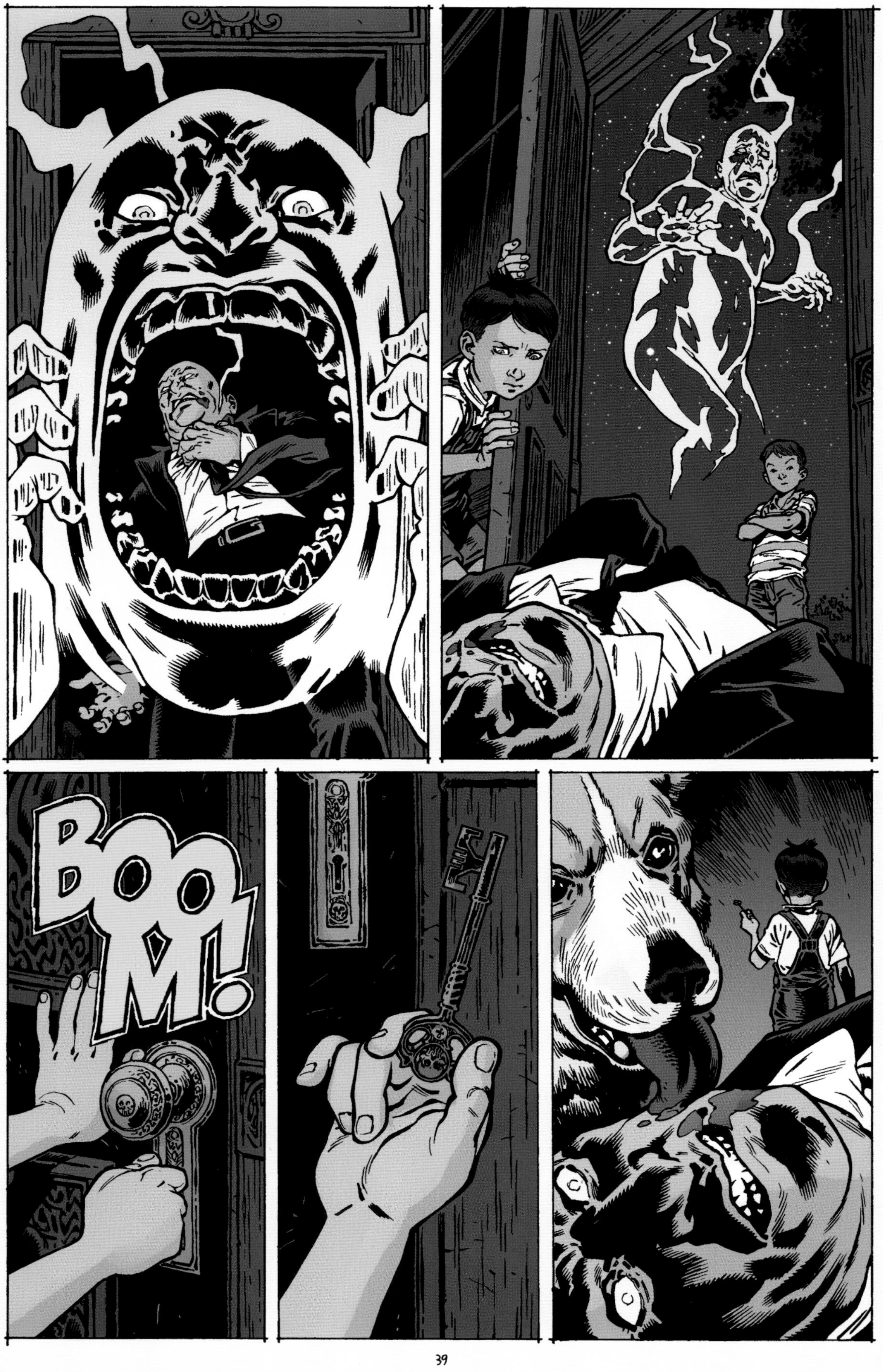
BOOM!

COME BACK ANYTIME. OUR DOOR IS ALWAYS OPEN.

CLAC!

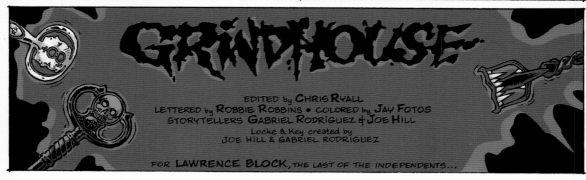

GRINDHOUSE

EDITED by CHRIS RYALL
LETTERED by ROBBIE ROBBINS • COLORED by JAY FOTOS
STORYTELLERS GABRIEL RODRÍGUEZ & JOE HILL
Locke & Key created by
JOE HILL & GABRIEL RODRÍGUEZ

FOR LAWRENCE BLOCK, THE LAST OF THE INDEPENDENTS...

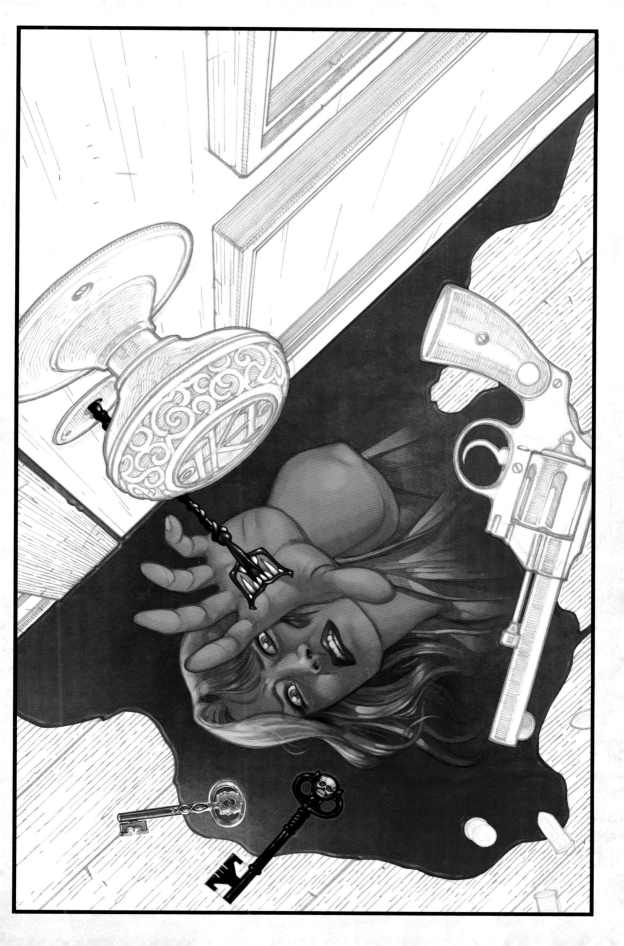

LOCKE & KEY: IN THE CAN

Written by Joe Hill
Art by Gabriel Rodríguez
Colors by Jay Fotos
Lettering by Robbins Robbins

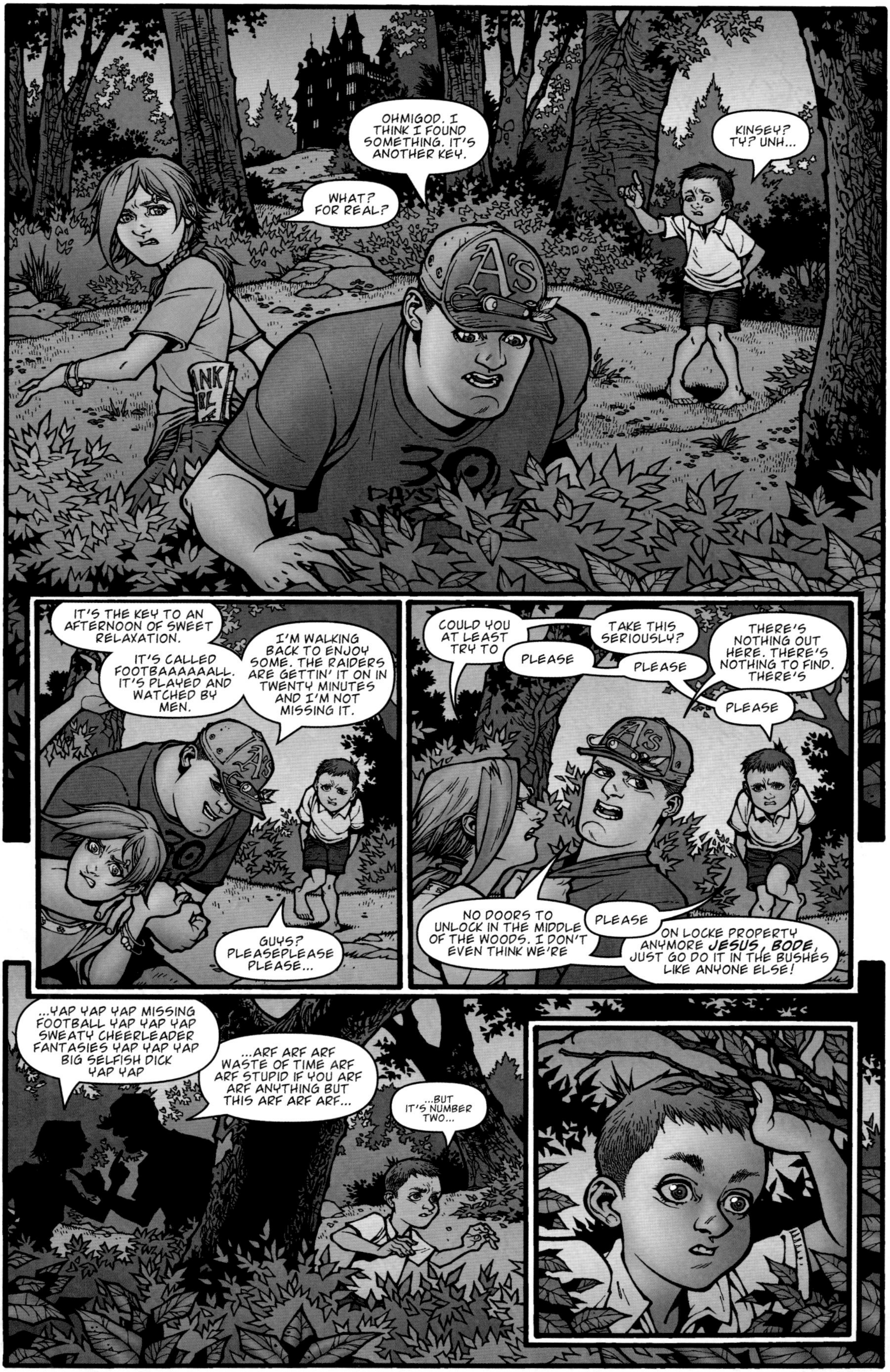
OHMIGOD. I THINK I FOUND SOMETHING. IT'S ANOTHER KEY.
WHAT? FOR REAL?
KINSEY? TY? UNH...
IT'S THE KEY TO AN AFTERNOON OF SWEET RELAXATION.
IT'S CALLED FOOTBAAAAAALL. IT'S PLAYED AND WATCHED BY MEN.
I'M WALKING BACK TO ENJOY SOME. THE RAIDERS ARE GETTIN' IT ON IN TWENTY MINUTES AND I'M NOT MISSING IT.
GUYS? PLEASEPLEASE PLEASE...
COULD YOU AT LEAST TRY TO
PLEASE
TAKE THIS SERIOUSLY?
PLEASE
THERE'S NOTHING OUT HERE. THERE'S NOTHING TO FIND. THERE'S
PLEASE
NO DOORS TO UNLOCK IN THE MIDDLE OF THE WOODS. I DON'T EVEN THINK WE'RE
PLEASE
ON LOCKE PROPERTY ANYMORE *JESUS, BODE*, JUST GO DO IT IN THE BUSHES LIKE ANYONE ELSE!
...YAP YAP YAP MISSING FOOTBALL YAP YAP YAP SWEATY CHEERLEADER FANTASIES YAP YAP YAP BIG SELFISH DICK YAP YAP
...ARF ARF ARF WASTE OF TIME ARF ARF STUPID IF YOU ARF ARF ANYTHING BUT THIS ARF ARF ARF...
...BUT IT'S NUMBER TWO...

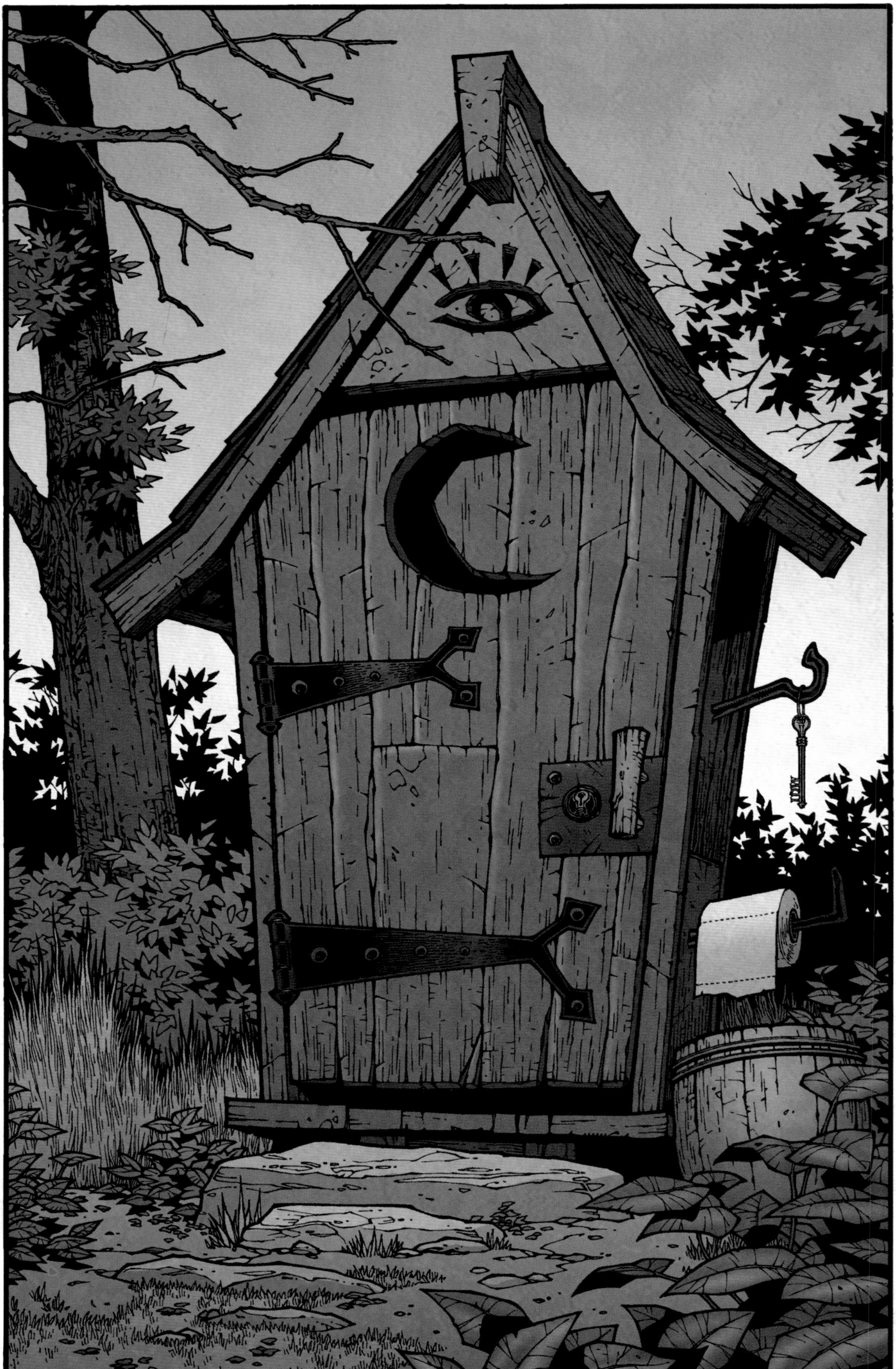

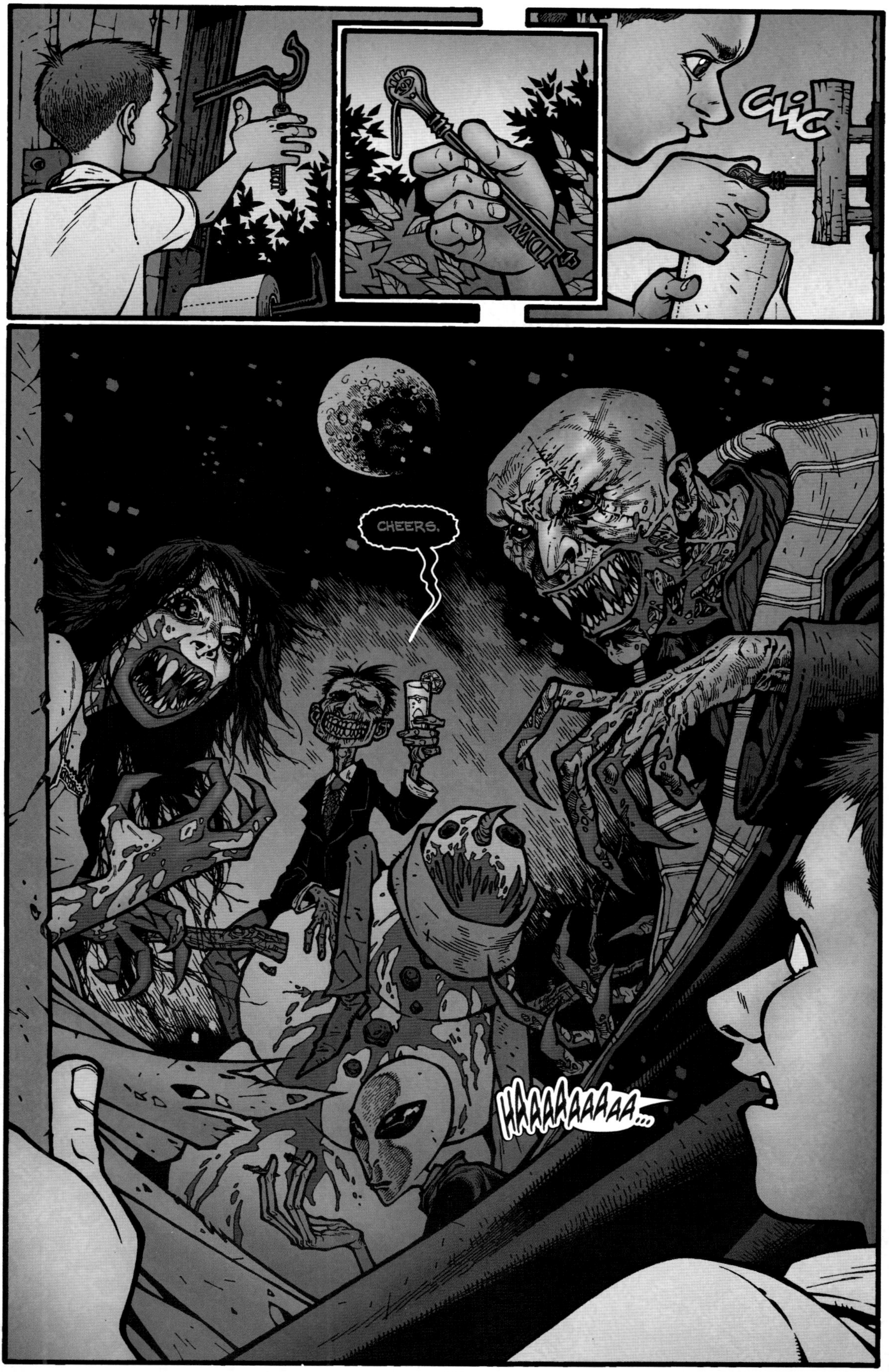
CLIC
CHEERS.
HAAAAAAAAA...

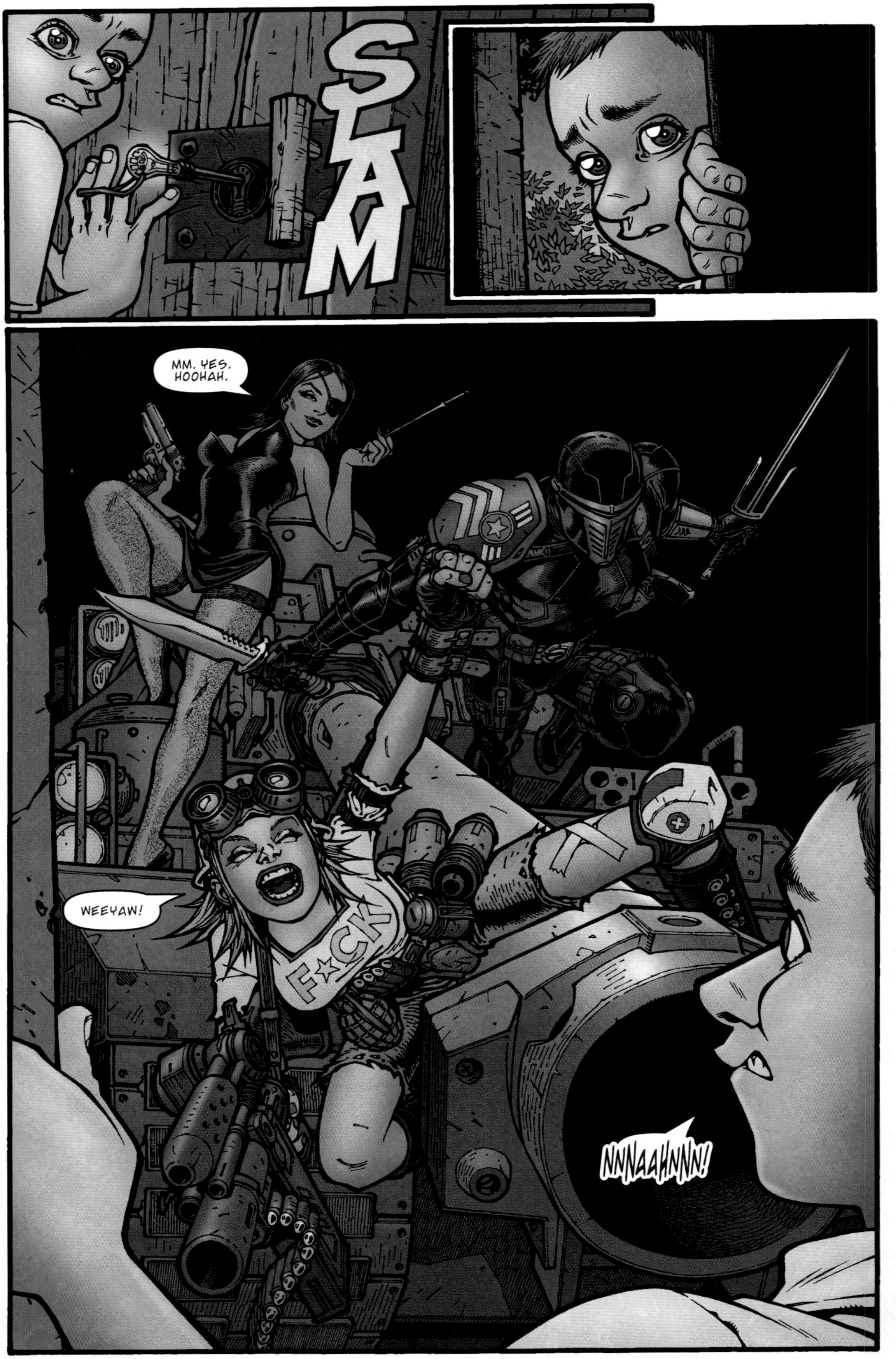
SLAM
MM. YES. HOOHAH.
F*CK
WEEYAW!
NNNAAHNNN!

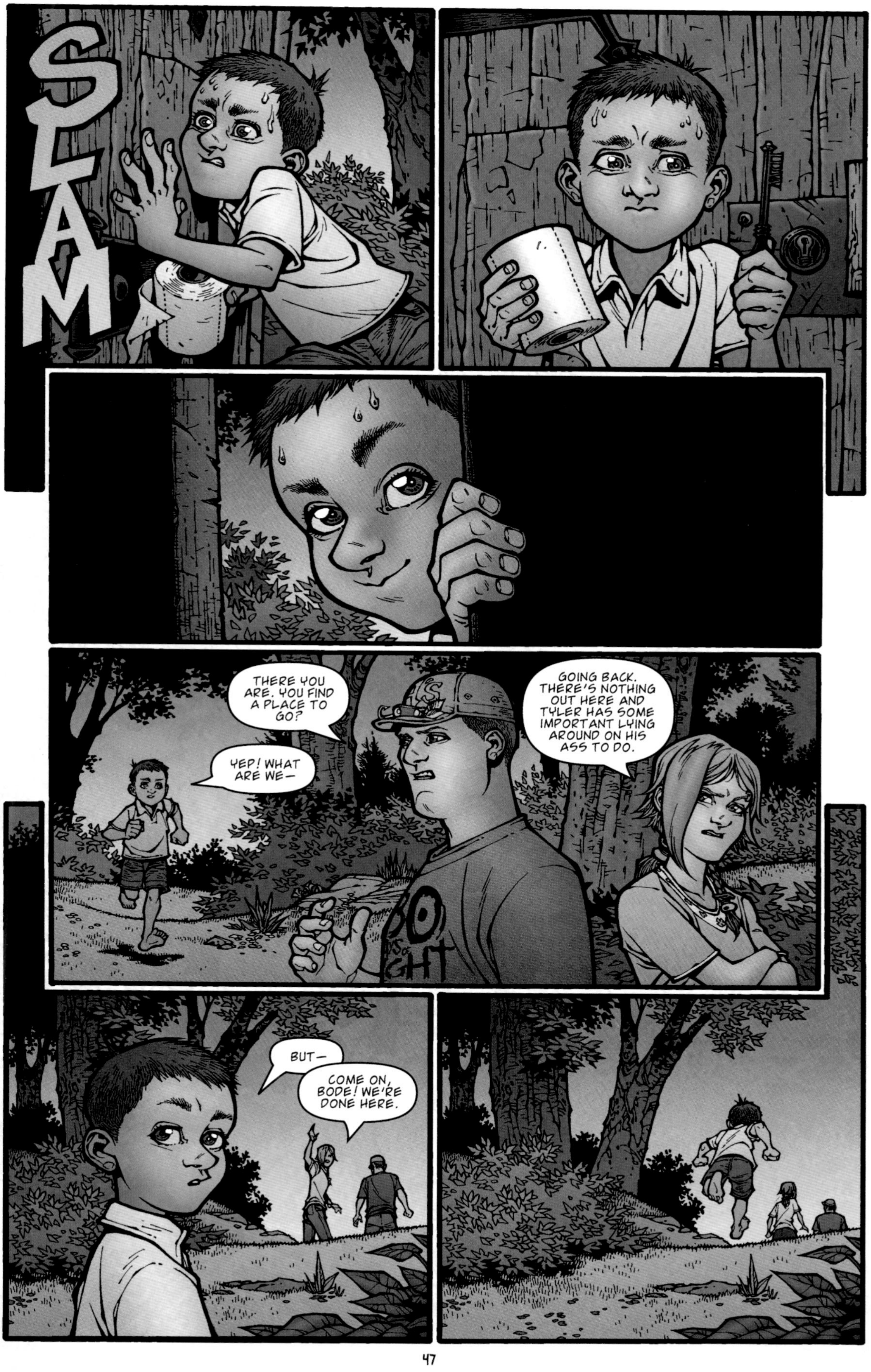
SLAM
THERE YOU ARE. YOU FIND A PLACE TO GO?
YEP! WHAT ARE WE—
GOING BACK. THERE'S NOTHING OUT HERE AND TYLER HAS SOME IMPORTANT LYING AROUND ON HIS ASS TO DO.
BUT—
COME ON, BODE! WE'RE DONE HERE.

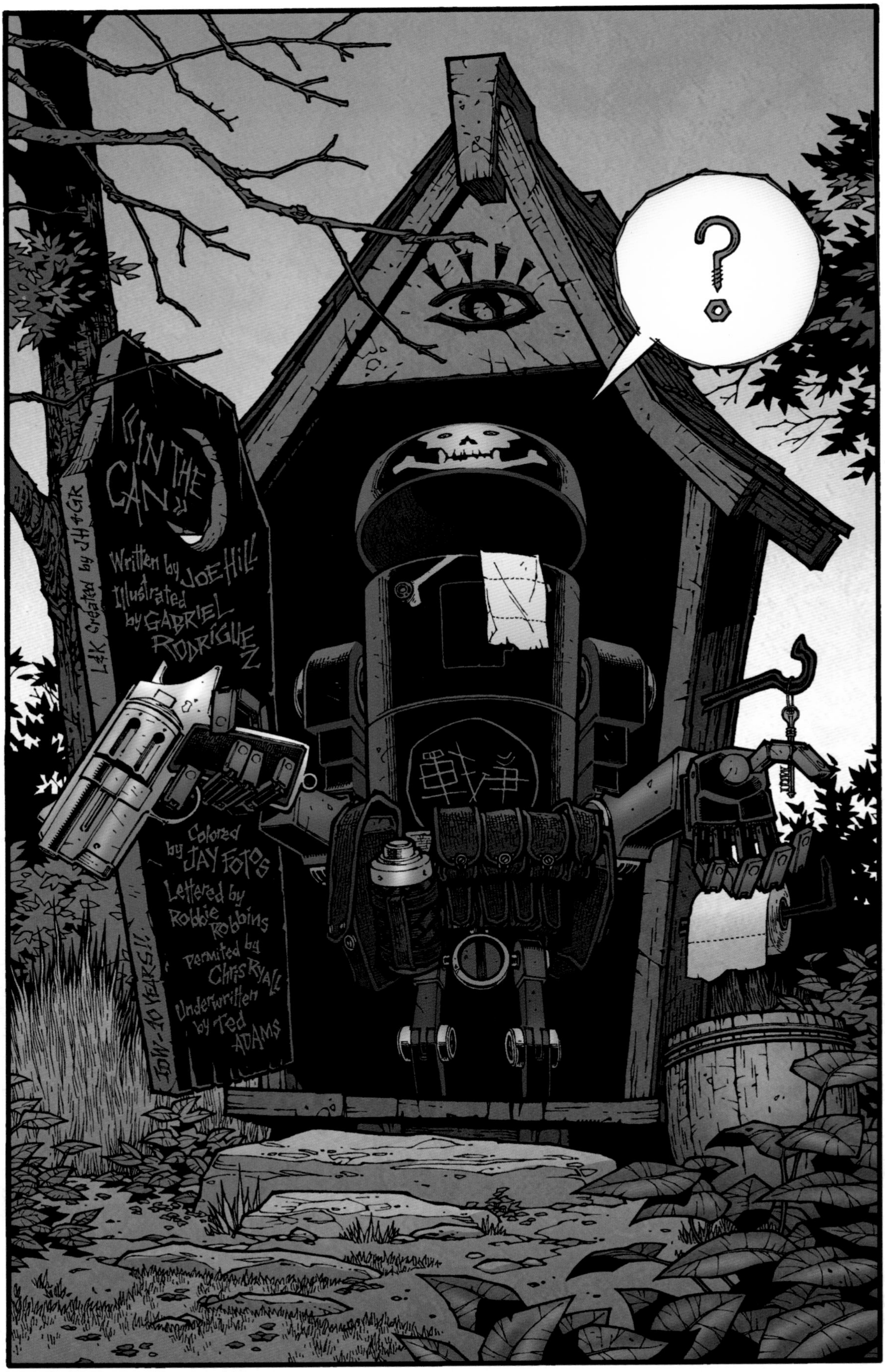
?
«IN THE CAN»
Written by JOE HILL
Illustrated by GABRIEL RODRIGUEZ
Colored by JAY FOTOS
Lettered by Robbie Robbins
Permited by Chris Ryall
Underwritten by Ted ADAMS
L&K Created by JH+GR
IDW-20 YEARS!!
戦争

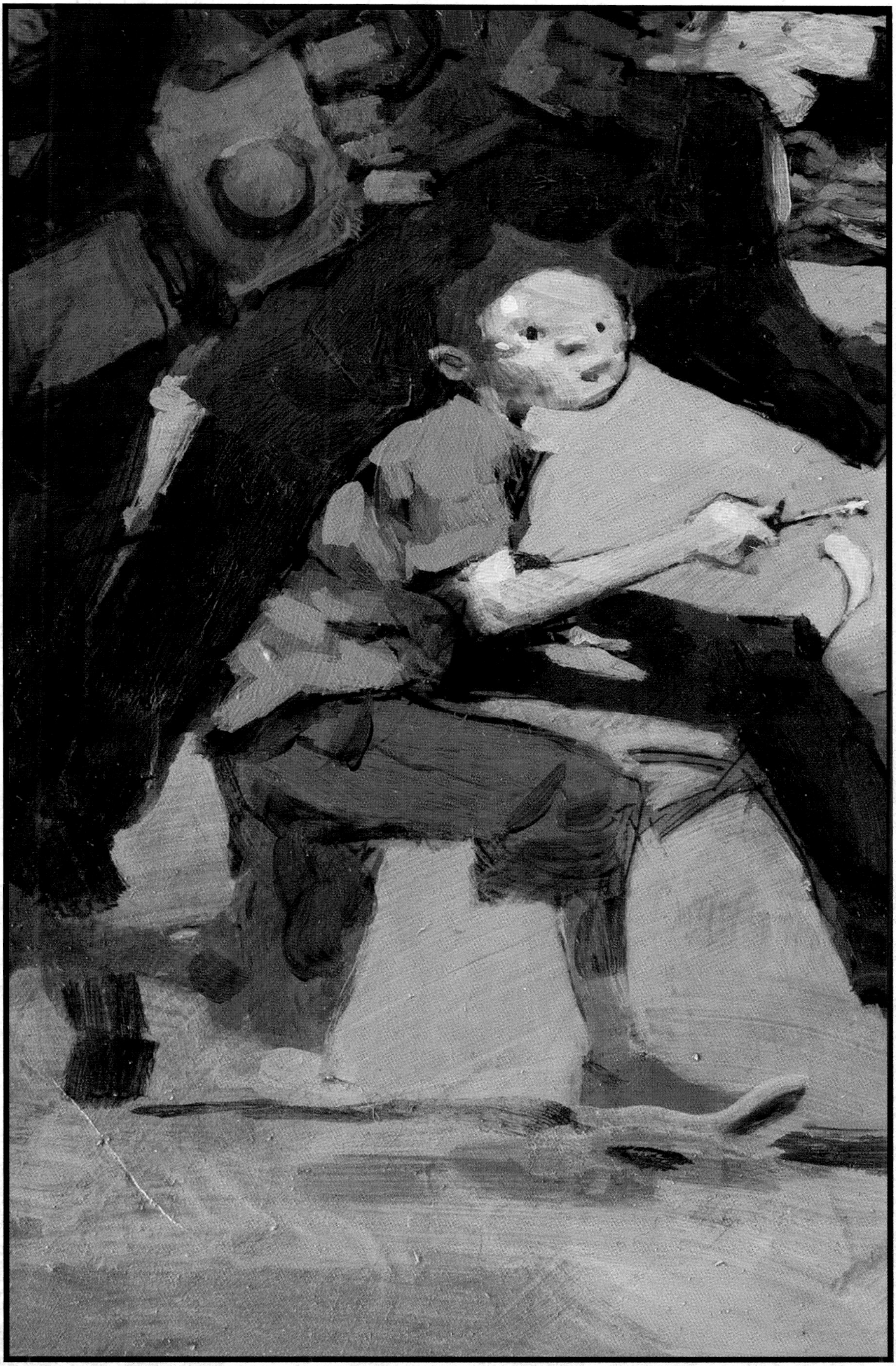

Art by Ashley Wood

THE REAL LOVECRAFT, MASS

In 2007, *Locke & Key* artist Gabriel Rodriguez created the visual map for Lovecraft, MA, based on Joe Hill's descriptions and some photo reference. Gabriel made the town an integral part of the story's visuals. Lovecraft might be a fictional place but its look and location were based on real haunts in Massachusetts. Even the book's "Drowning Cave" was based on a real landmark, "Swallow Cave" in Nahant, Mass.

In August 2013, following a successful appearance at the Boston Comic-Con, Gabriel was able to see these locations in person for the first time. Joe Hill led an expedition in and around Nahant so Gabriel, along with Editor Chris Ryall, keymaker extraordinaire Israel Skelton, writer Jason Ciaramella, *Wraith* artist Charles P. Wilson

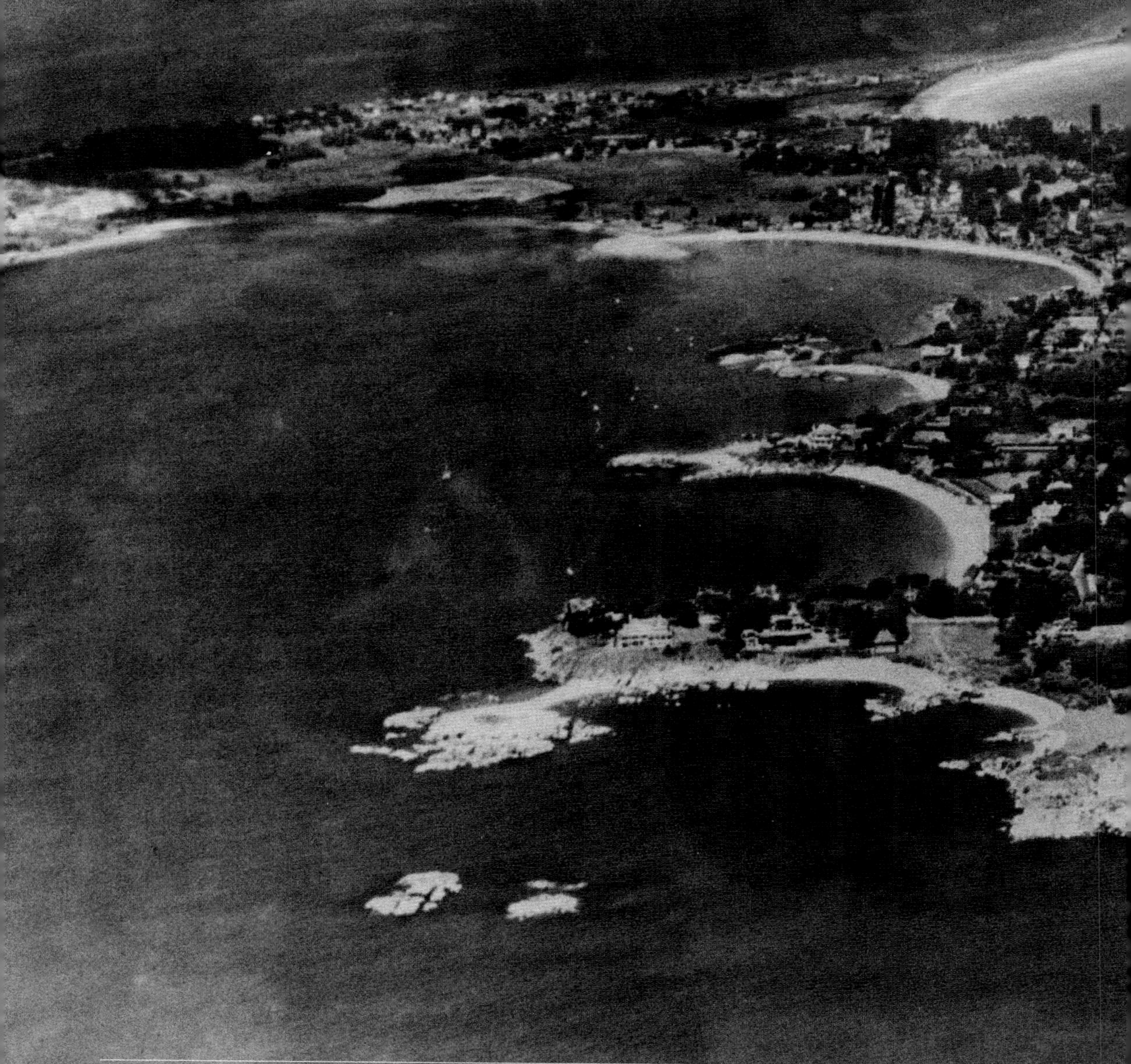

All photos for the following photo essay are by Shane Leonard unless otherwise noted.

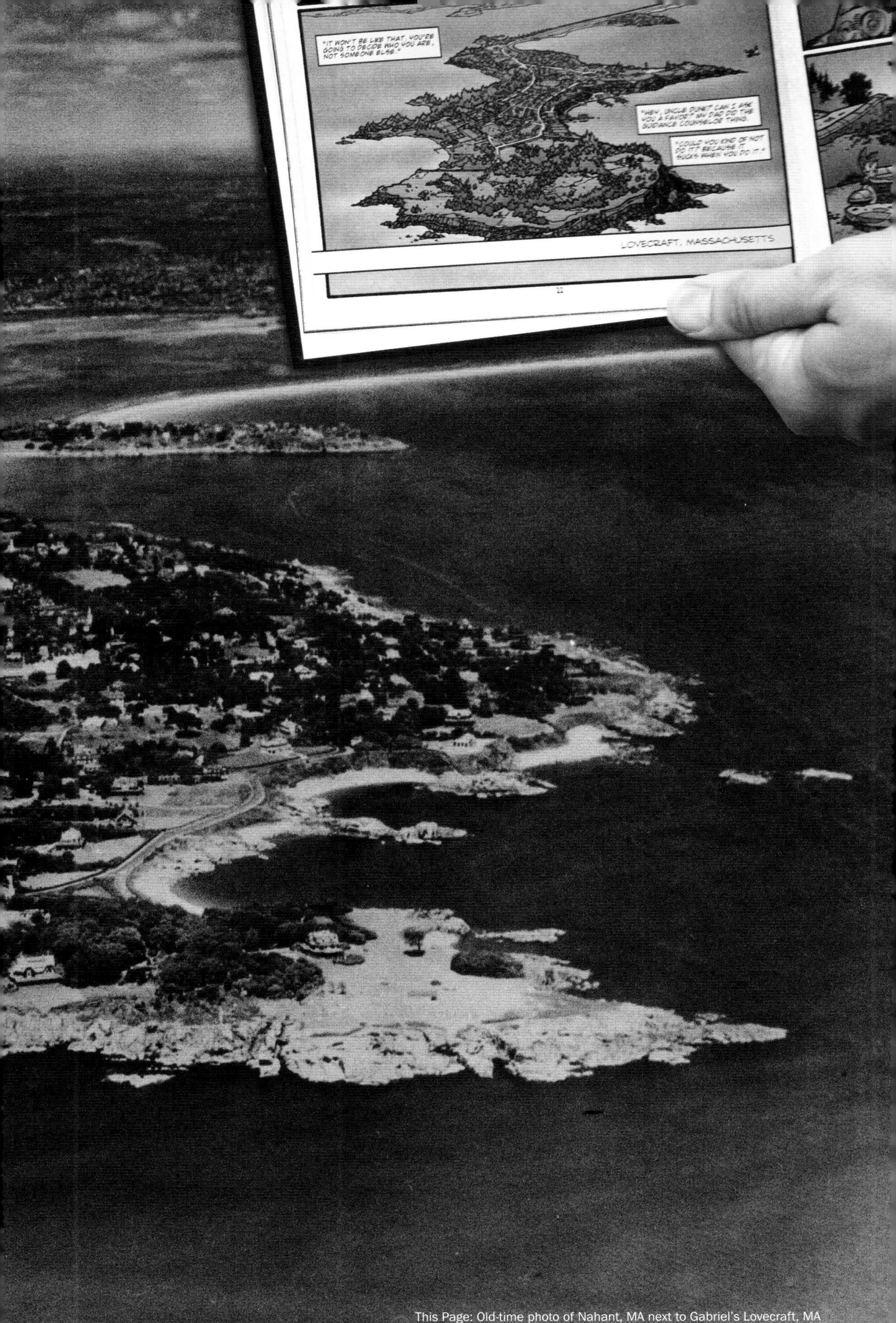
"IT WON'T BE LIKE THAT. YOU'RE GOING TO DECIDE WHO YOU ARE, NOT SOMEONE ELSE."
"HEY, UNCLE DUNK! CAN I ASK YOU A FAVOR? MY DAD DID THE GUIDANCE COUNSELOR THING."
"COULD YOU KIND OF NOT DO IT? BECAUSE IT SUCKS WHEN YOU DO IT."
LOVECRAFT, MASSACHUSETTS
11

This Page: Old-time photo of Nahant, MA next to Gabriel's Lovecraft, MA

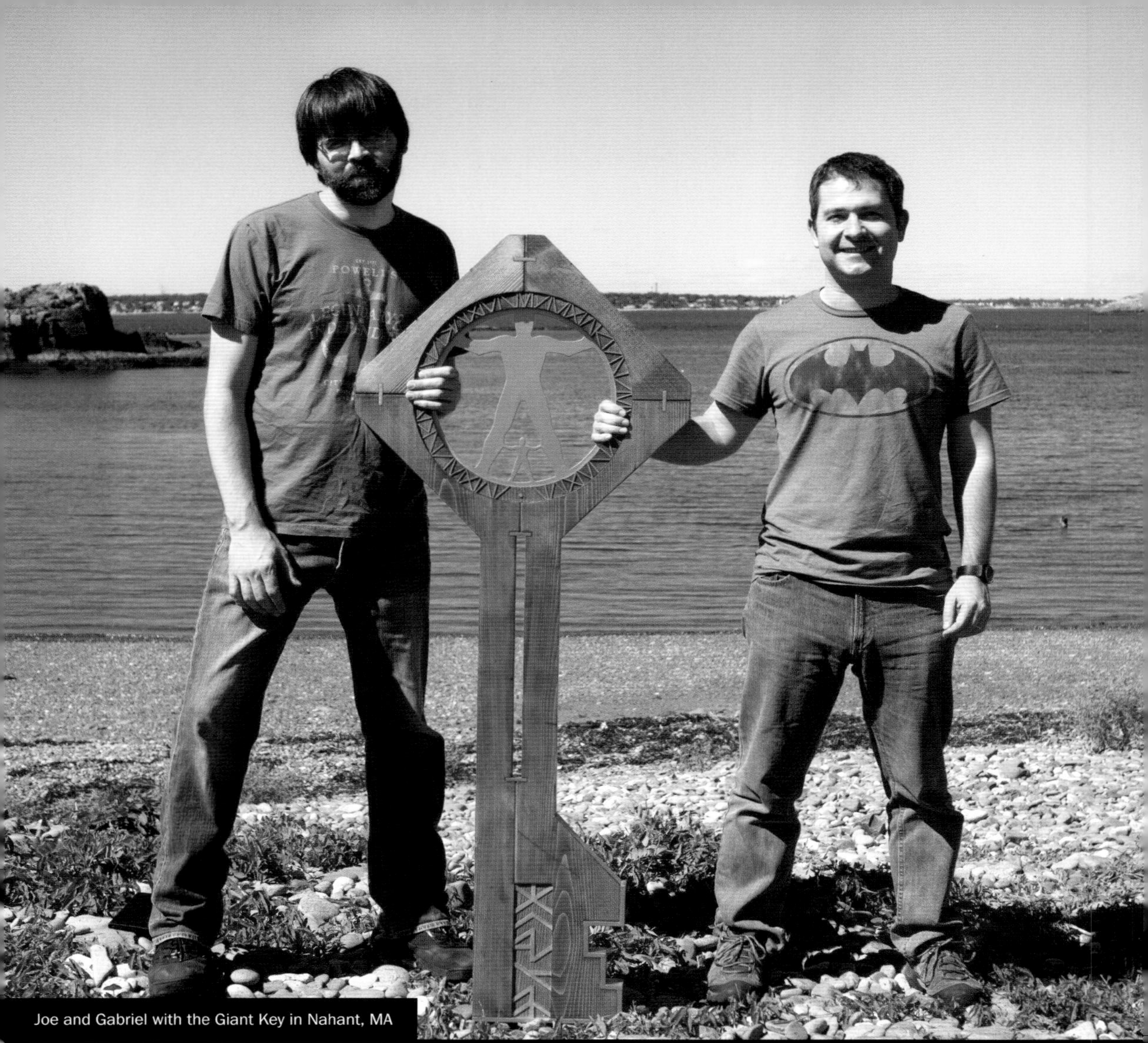
Joe and Gabriel with the Giant Key in Nahant, MA

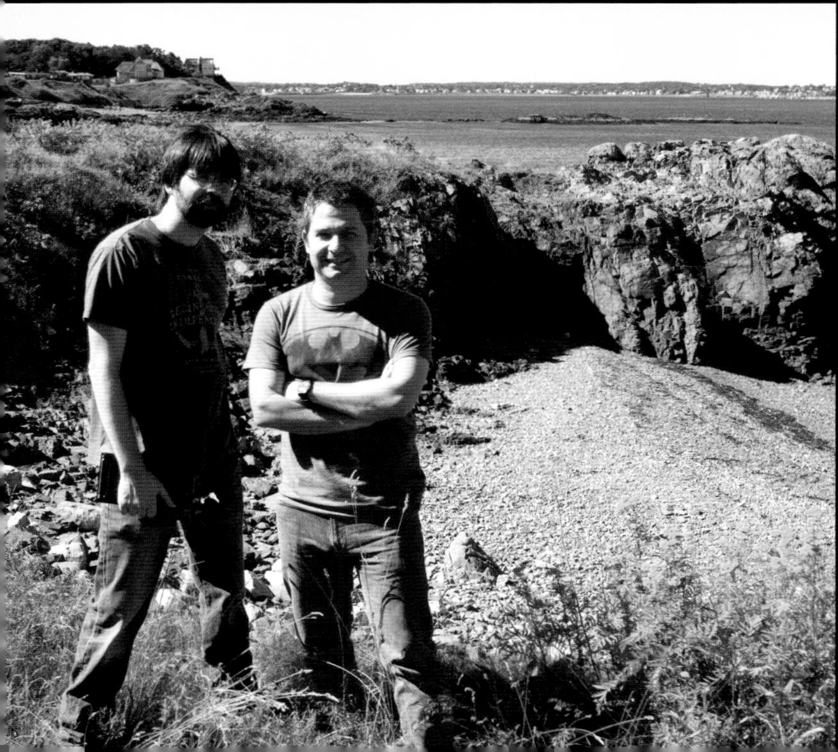

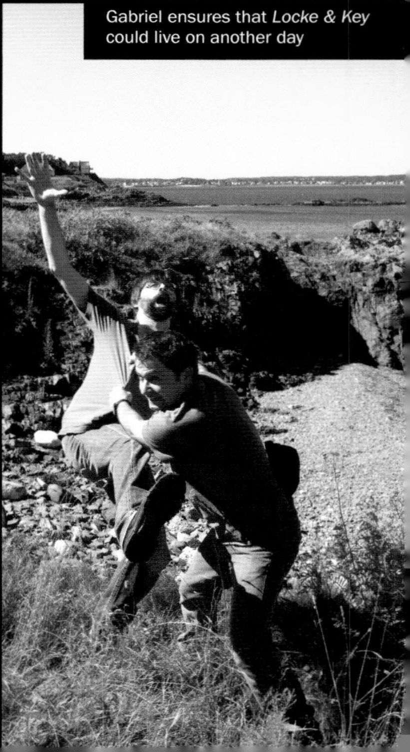
Gabriel ensures that *Locke & Key* could live on another day

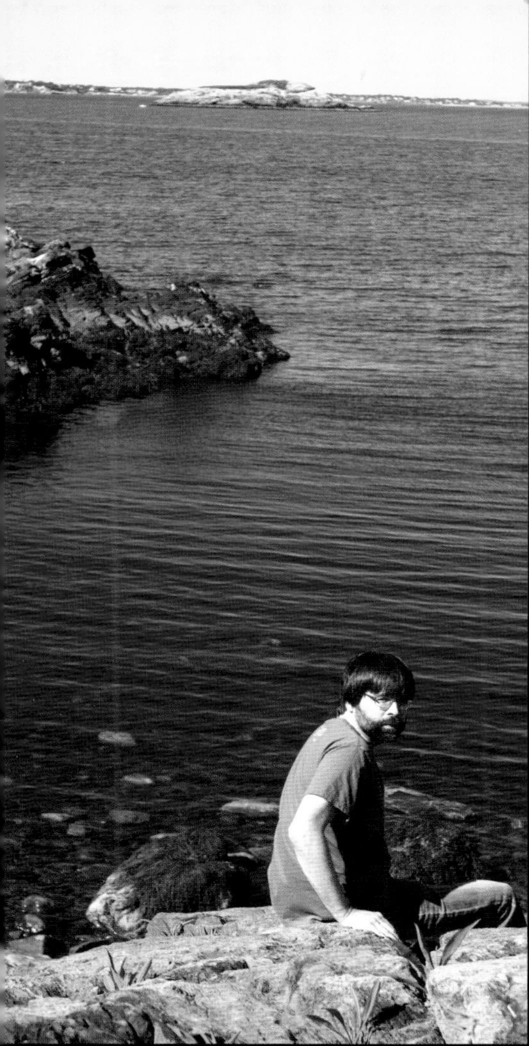

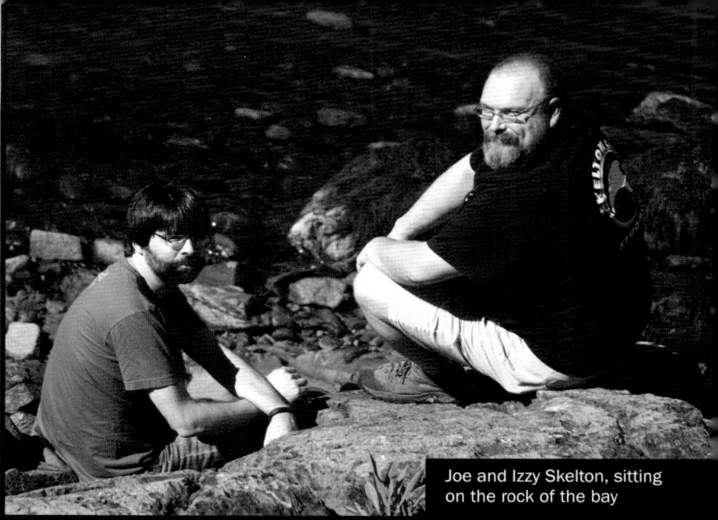

Joe and Izzy Skelton, sitting on the rock of the bay

Chris Ryall and Joe Hill

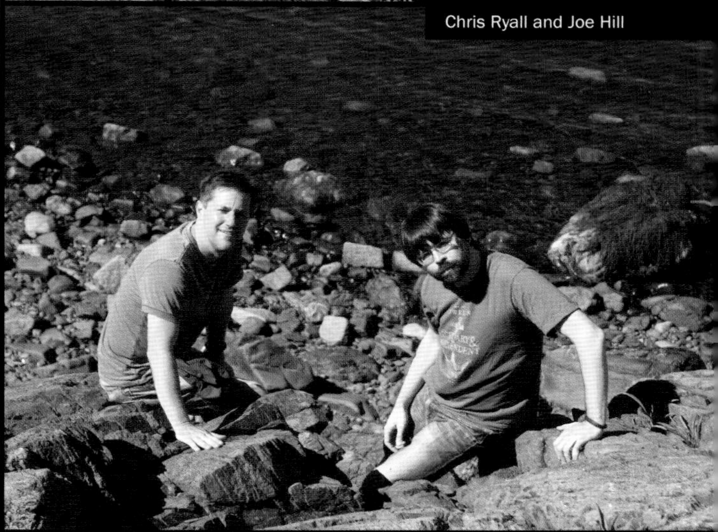

Joe and Gabriel sit on rocks that Gabriel has been drawing for years

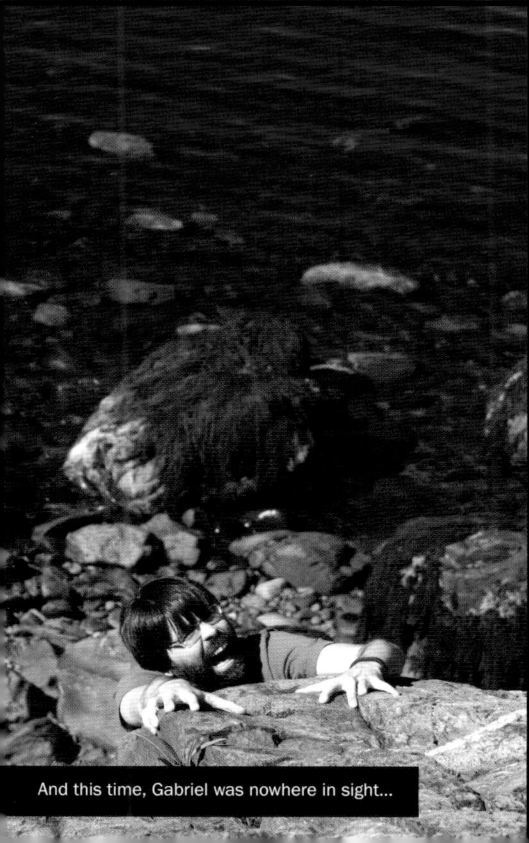

And this time, Gabriel was nowhere in sight...

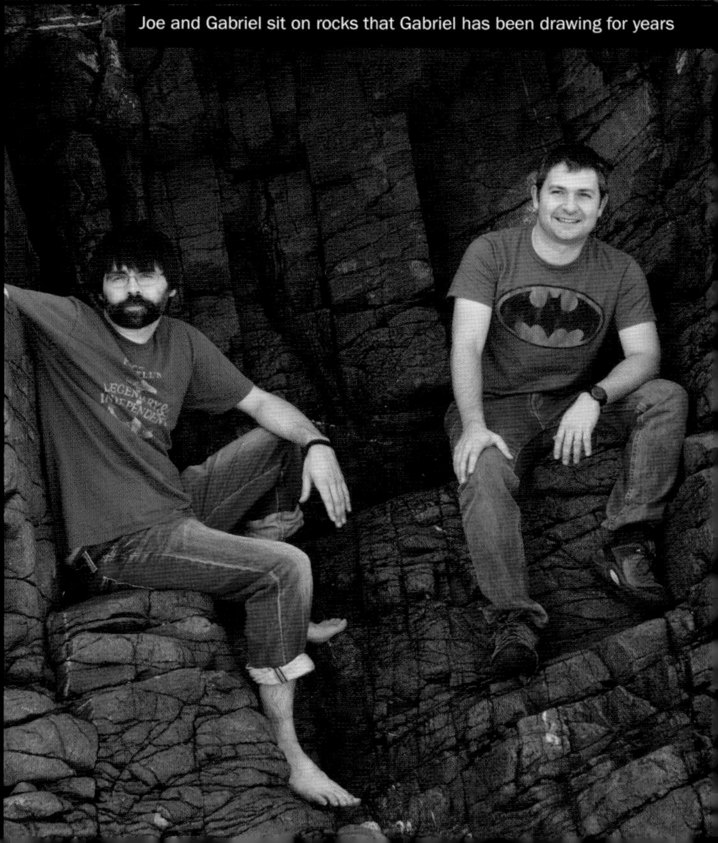

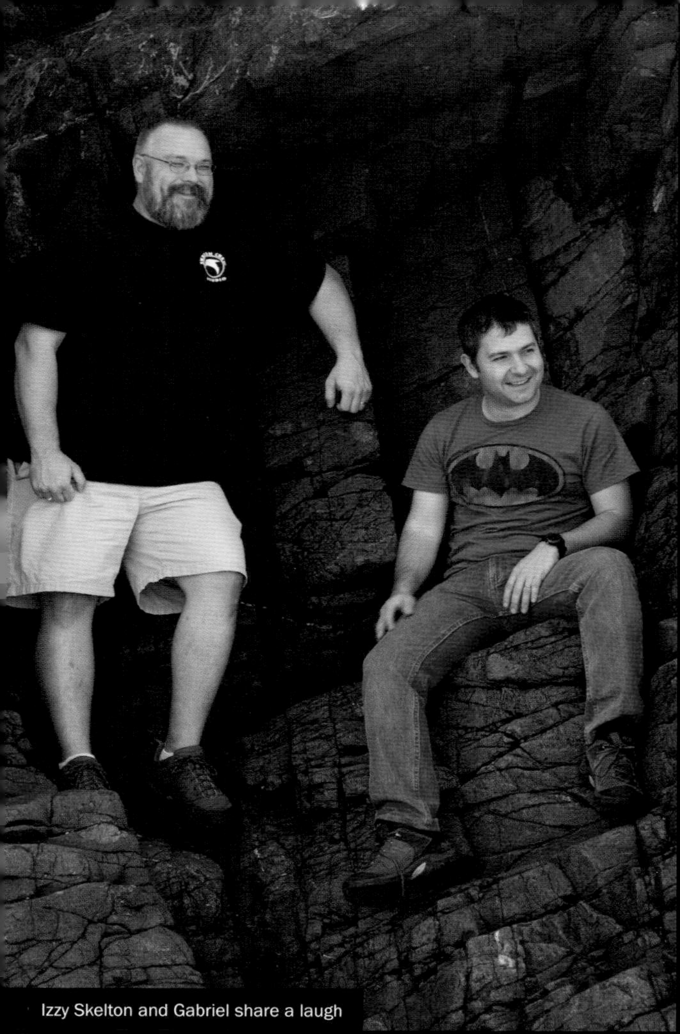

Izzy Skelton and Gabriel share a laugh

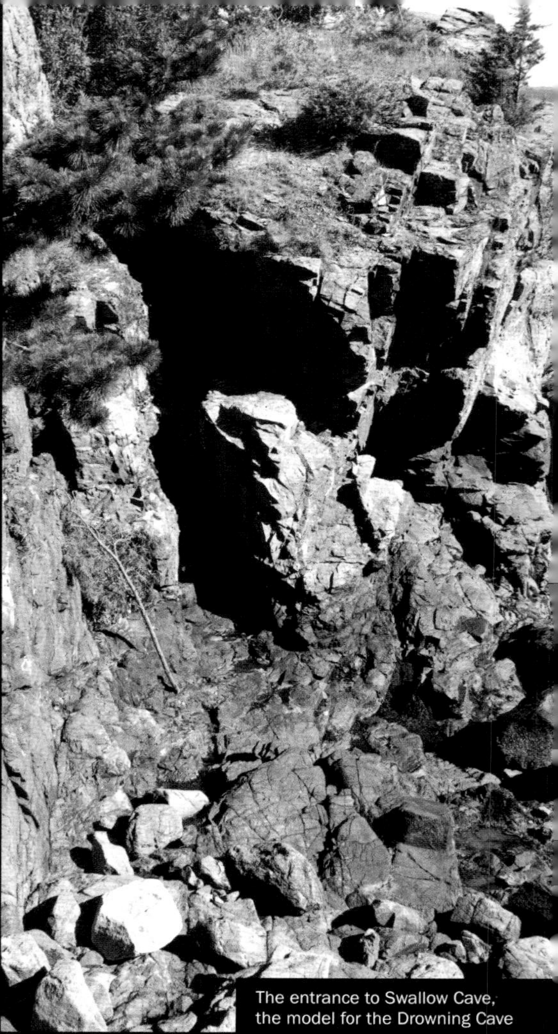

The entrance to Swallow Cave, the model for the Drowning Cave

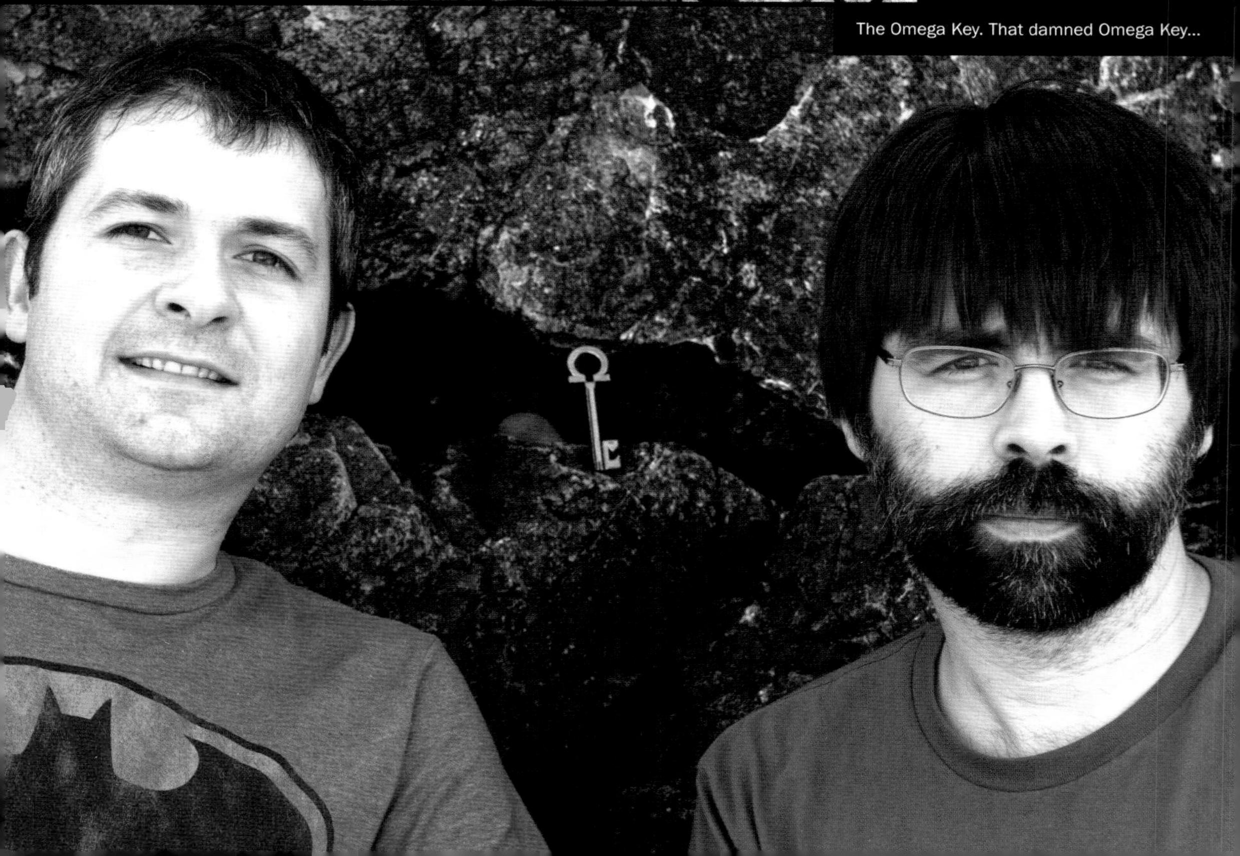

The Omega Key. That damned Omega Key...

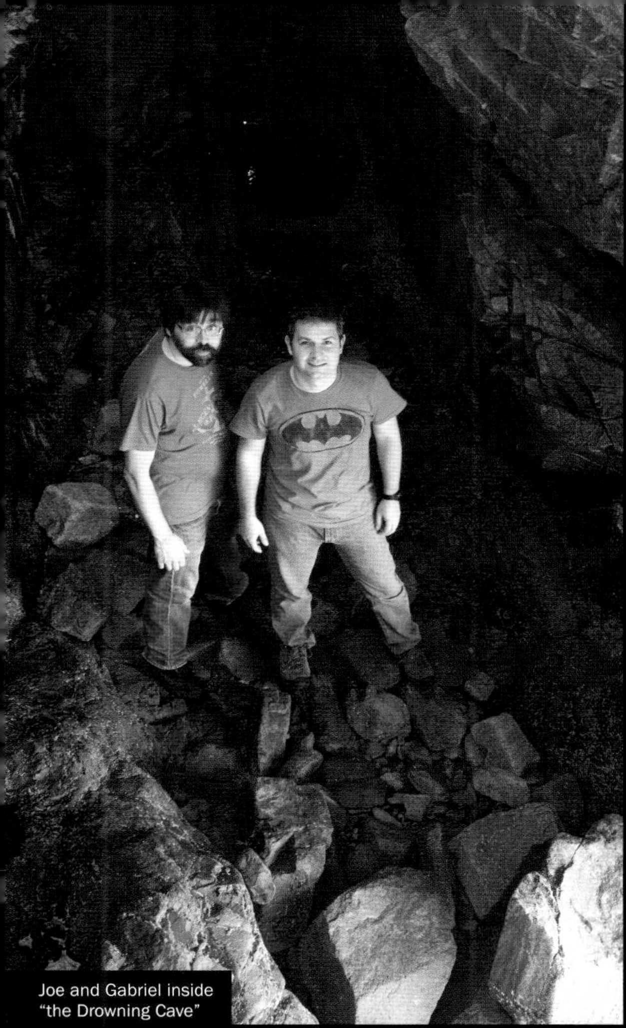

Joe and Gabriel inside "the Drowning Cave"

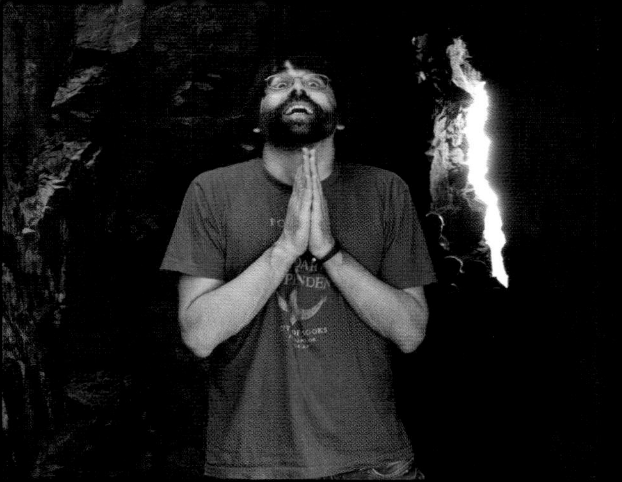

Joe prays this day ends better for him than the "Cave Rave" in his comic

Joe and Gabriel at the crossroads of "Drowning Cave Road"

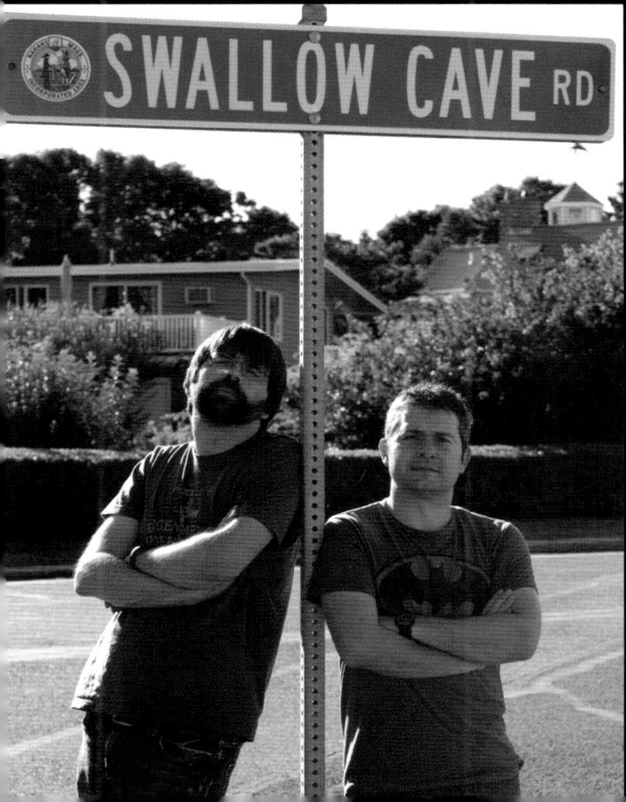
SWALLOW CAVE RD

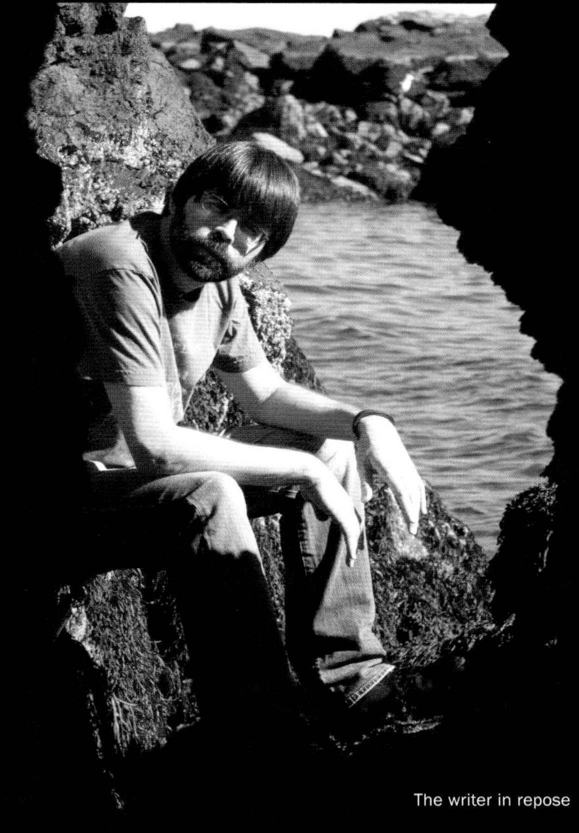

The writer in repose

If you didn't like the ending of this series, well...

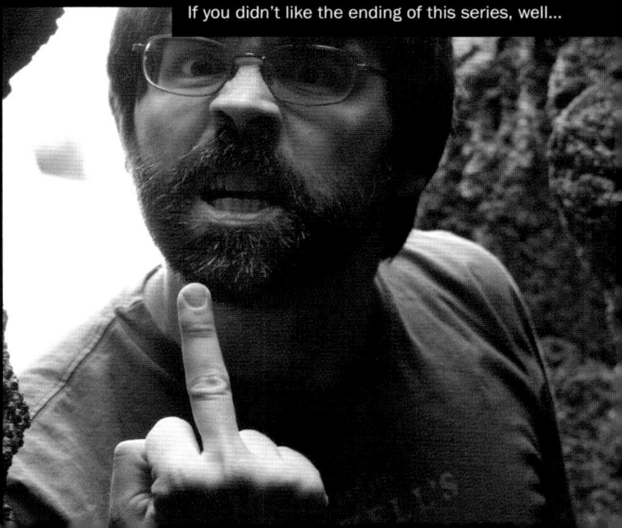

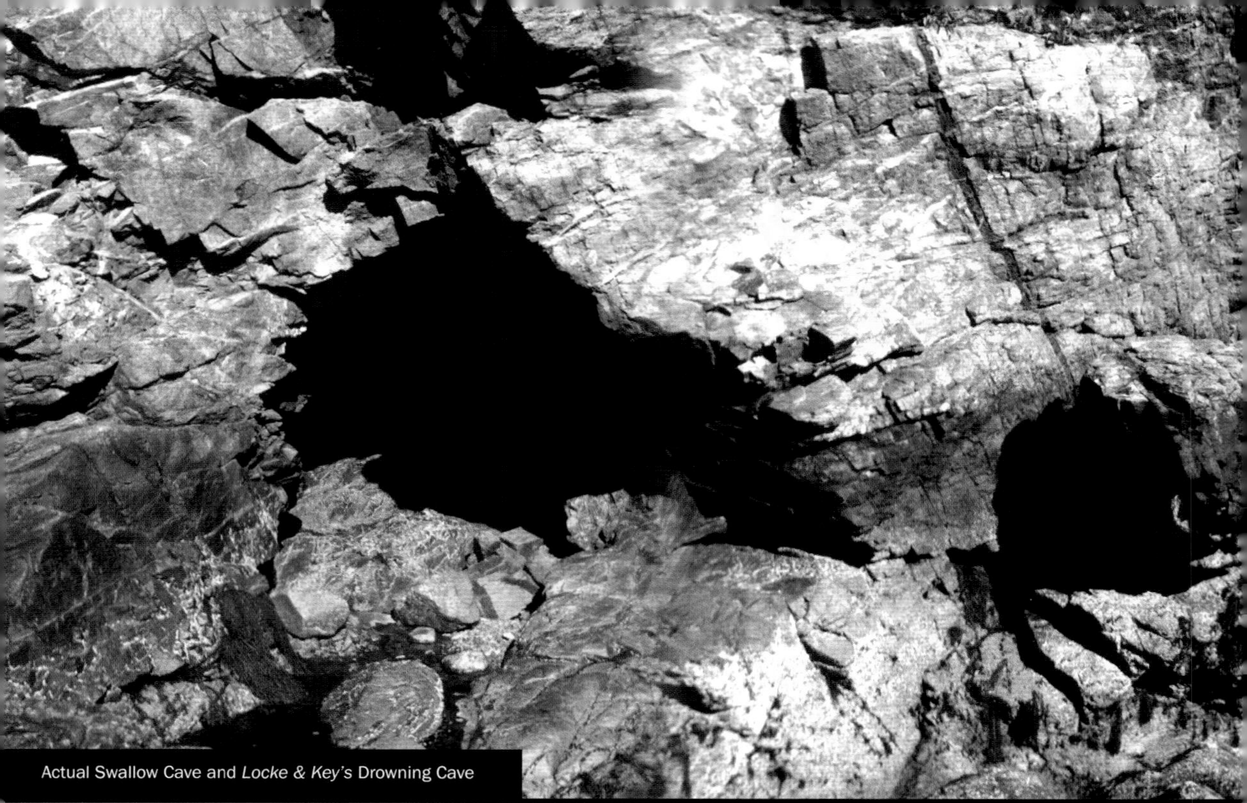

Actual Swallow Cave and *Locke & Key's* Drowning Cave

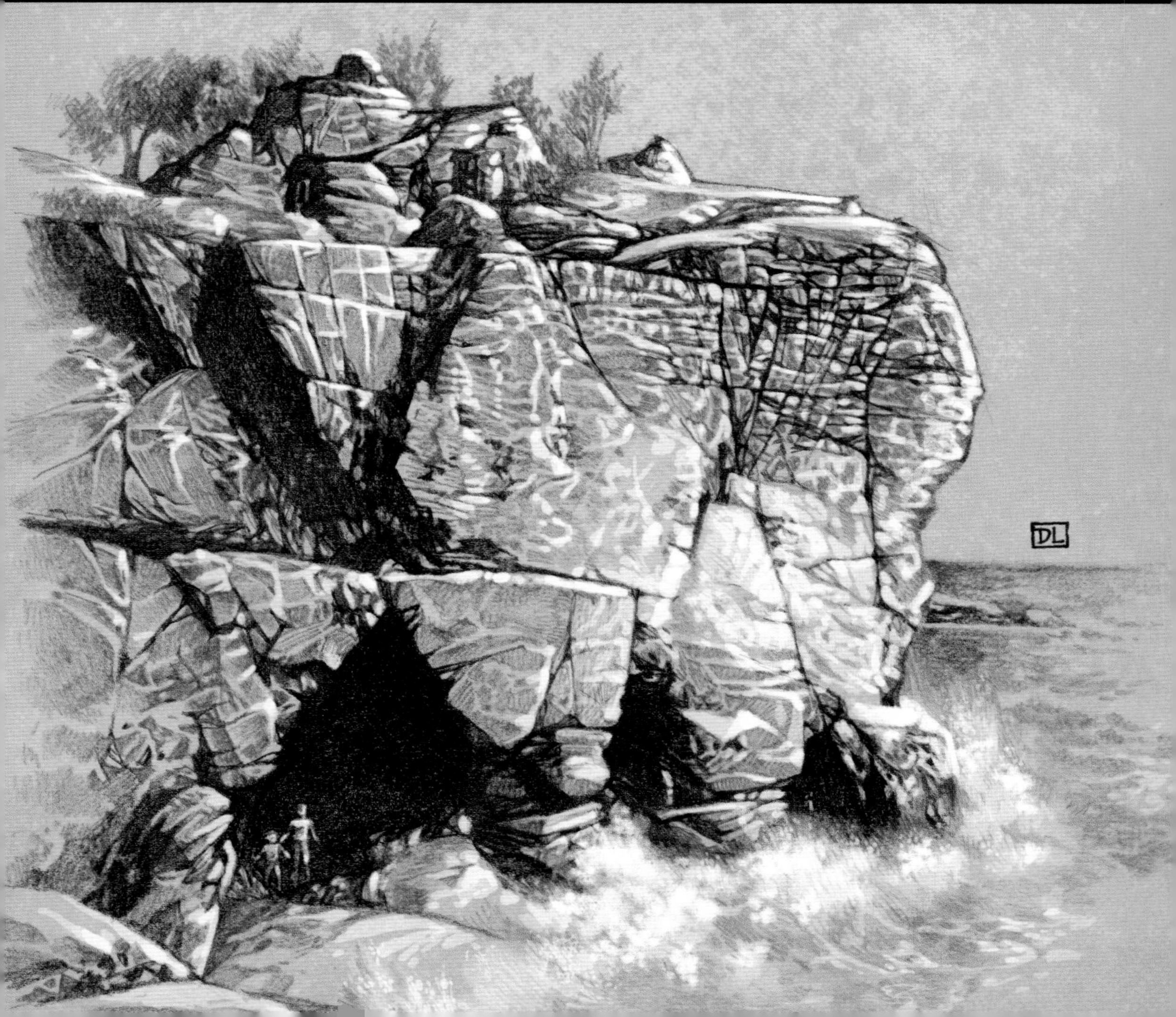

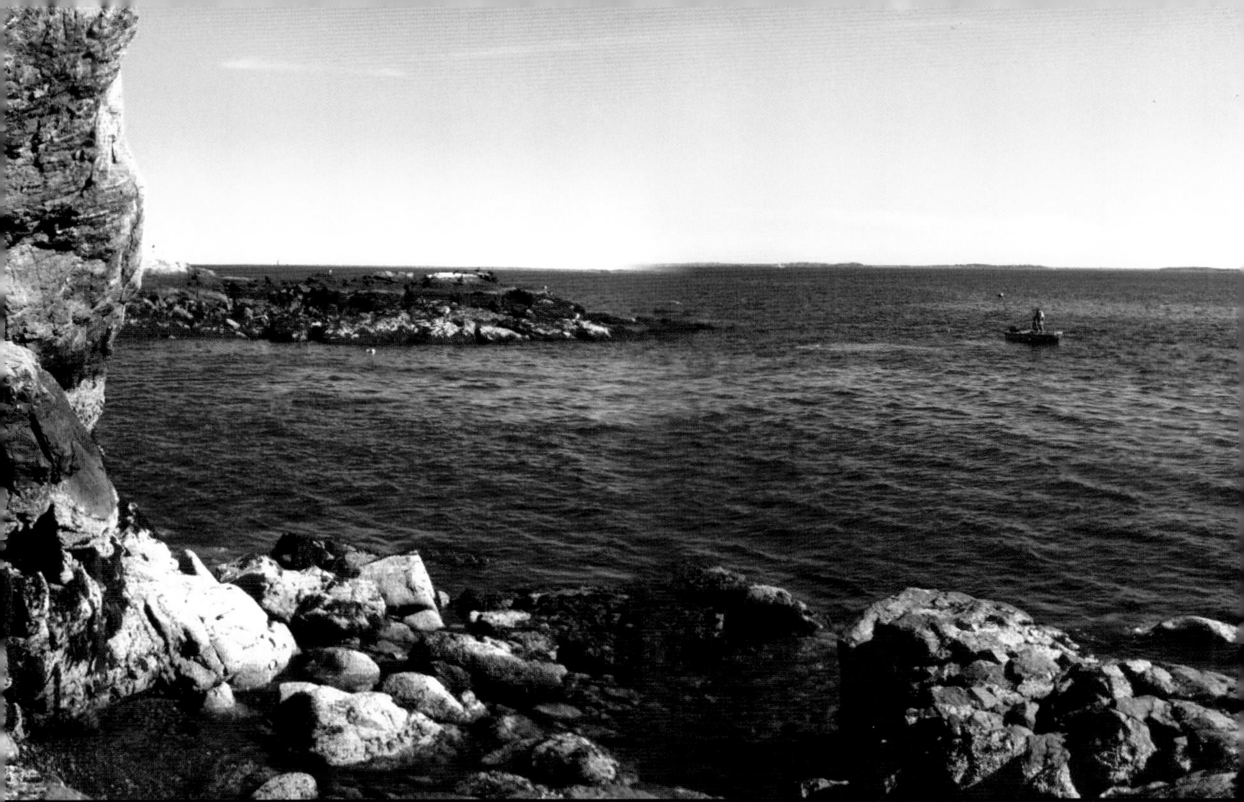

Chris Ryall, Joe Hill, and Gabriel Rodriguez at the mouth of the cave

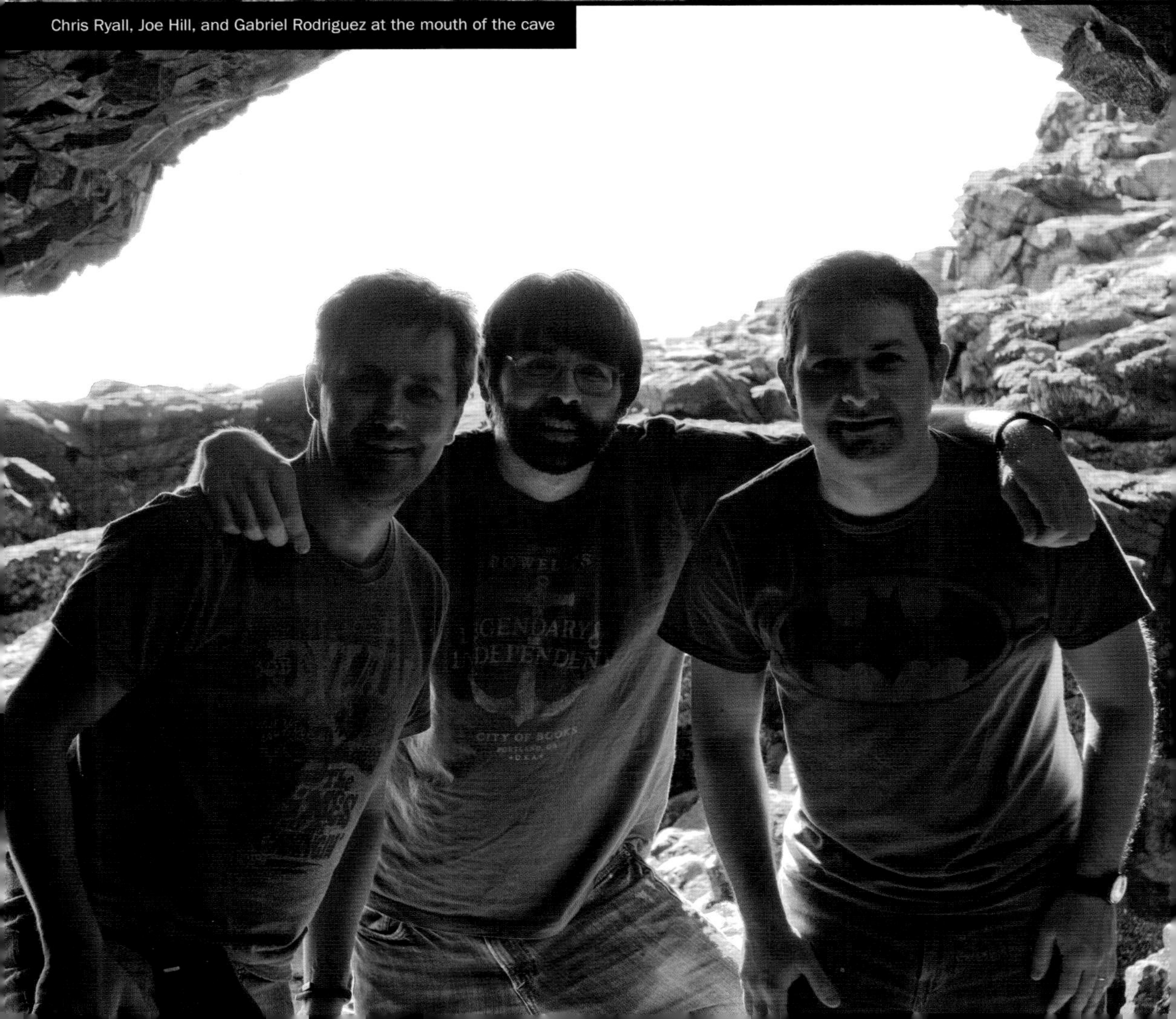
CITY OF BOOKS

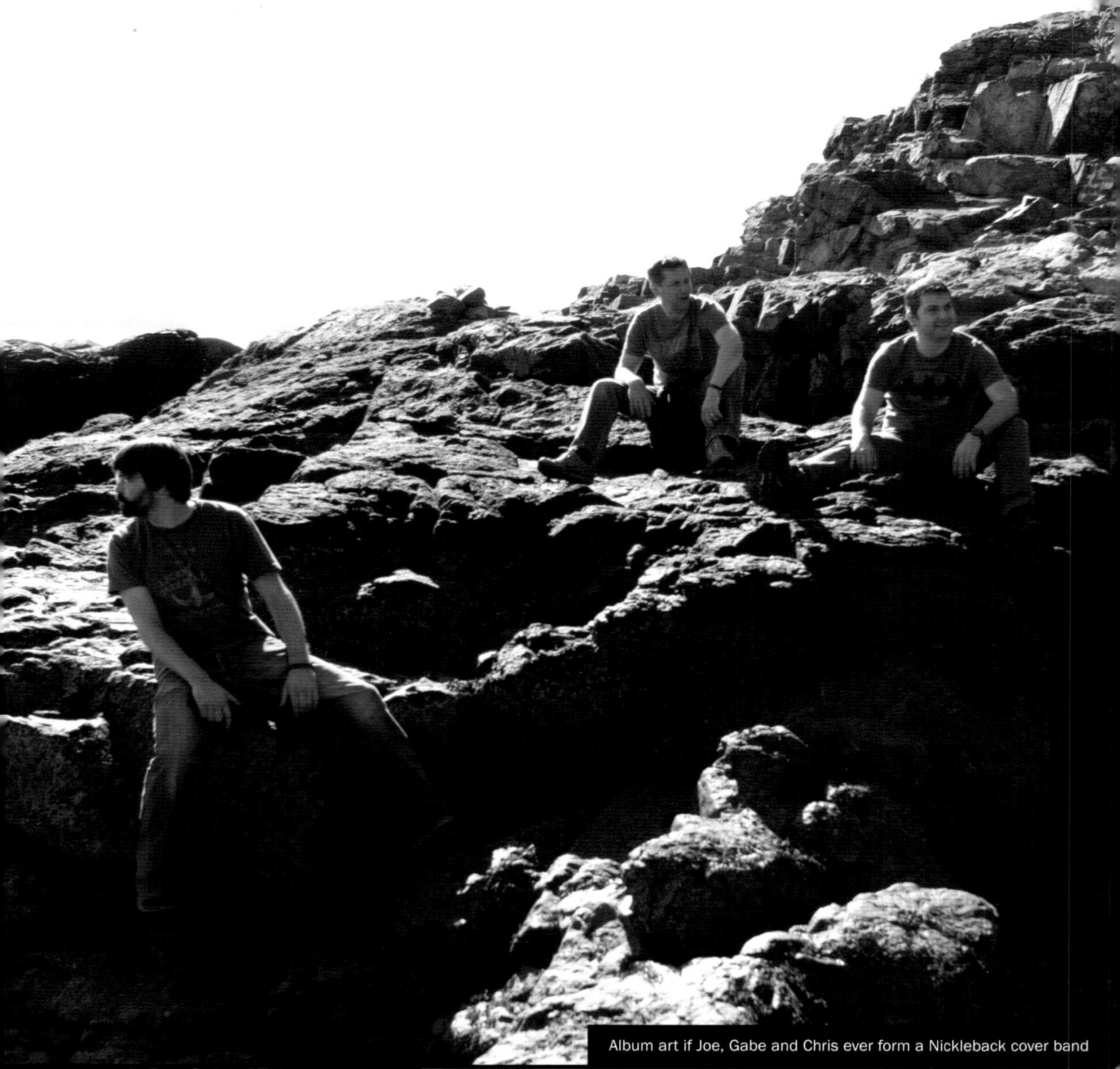

Album art if Joe, Gabe and Chris ever form a Nickleback cover band

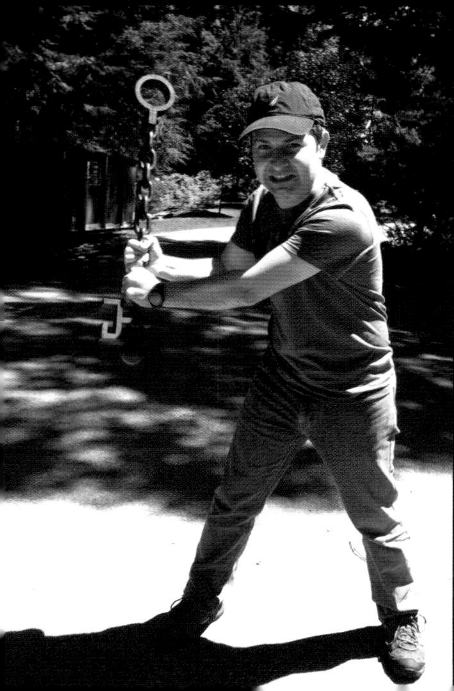

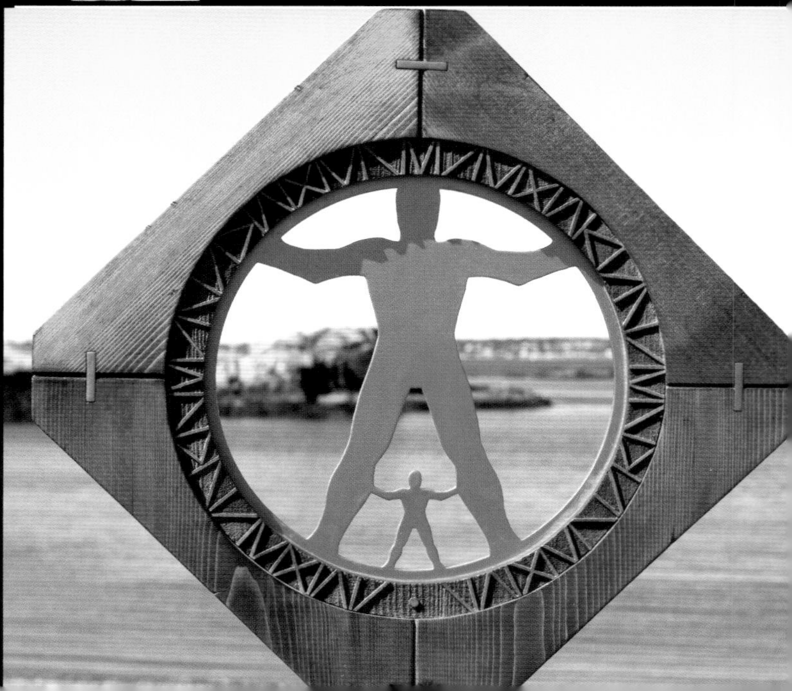

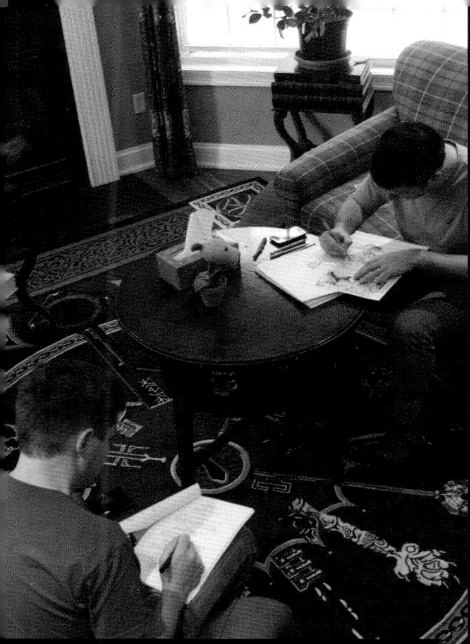

Chris and Gabriel find inspiration in Joe's Reading Room, complete with *Locke & Key* rug

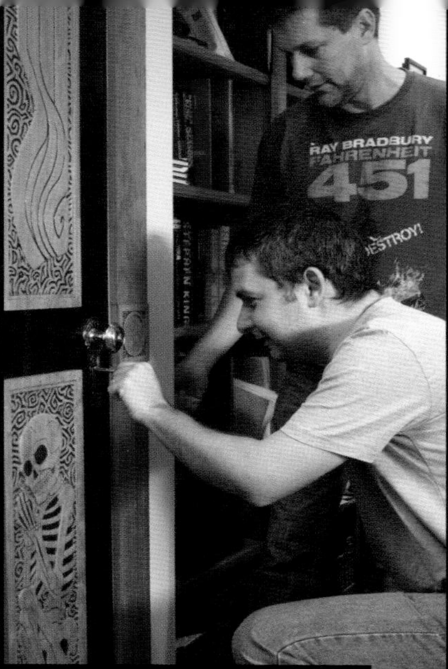
RAY BRADBURY
FAHRENHEIT
451

Gabriel and Chris use the Ghost Key to open Joe's working Ghost Door

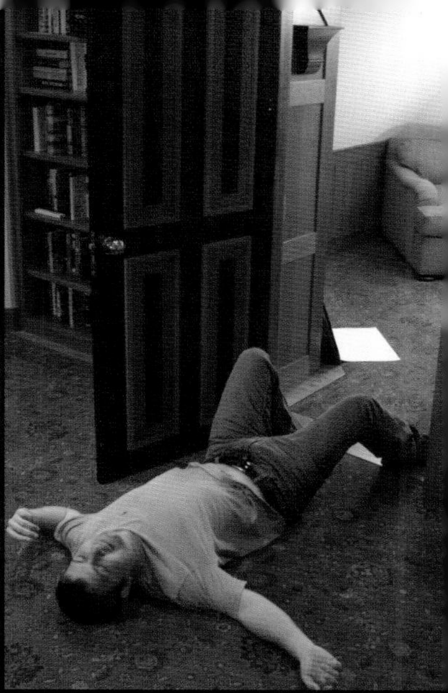

After 45 issues of *Locke & Key,* Gabriel earns the sweet release the Ghost Door offers

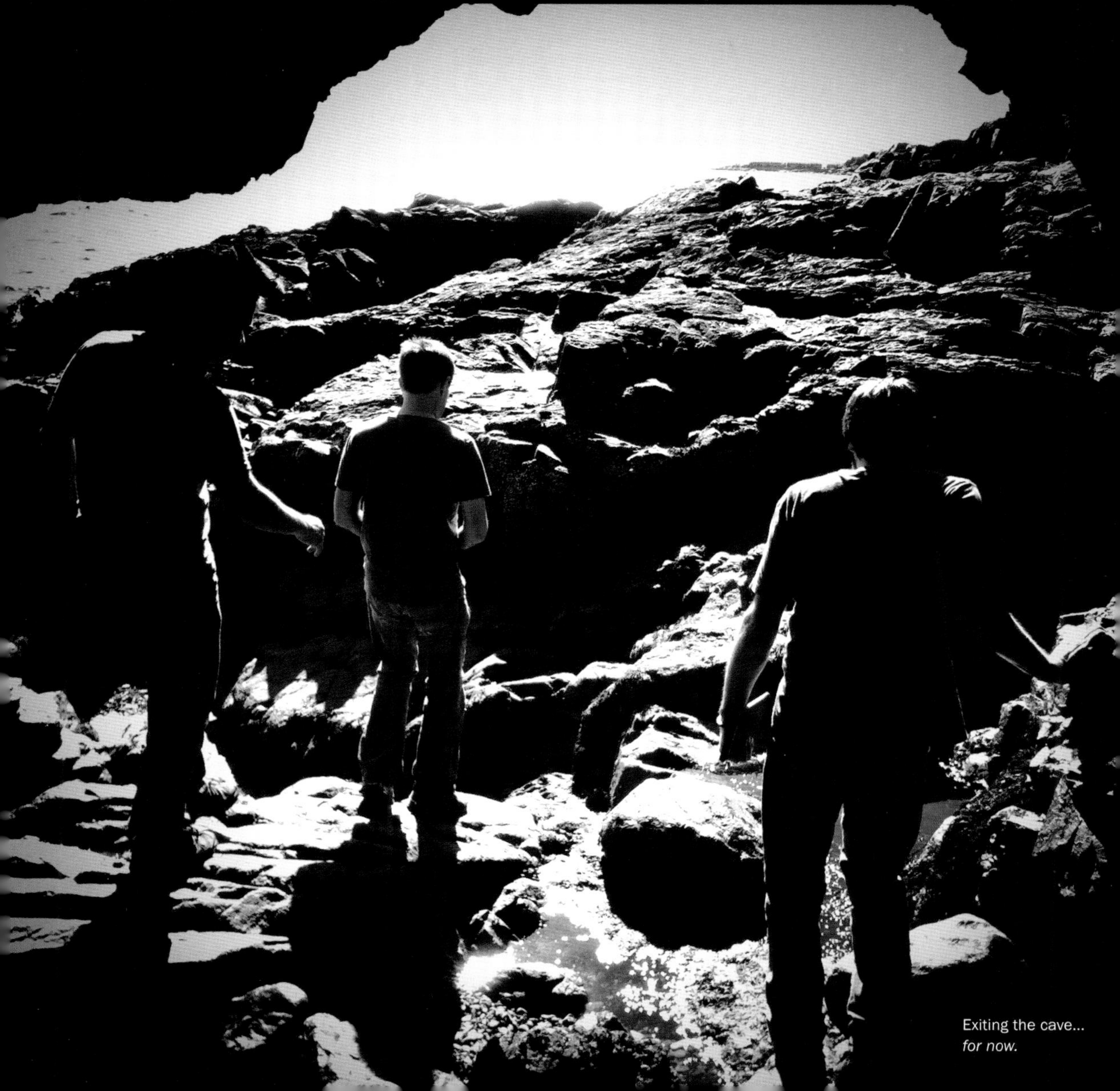

Exiting the cave...
for now.

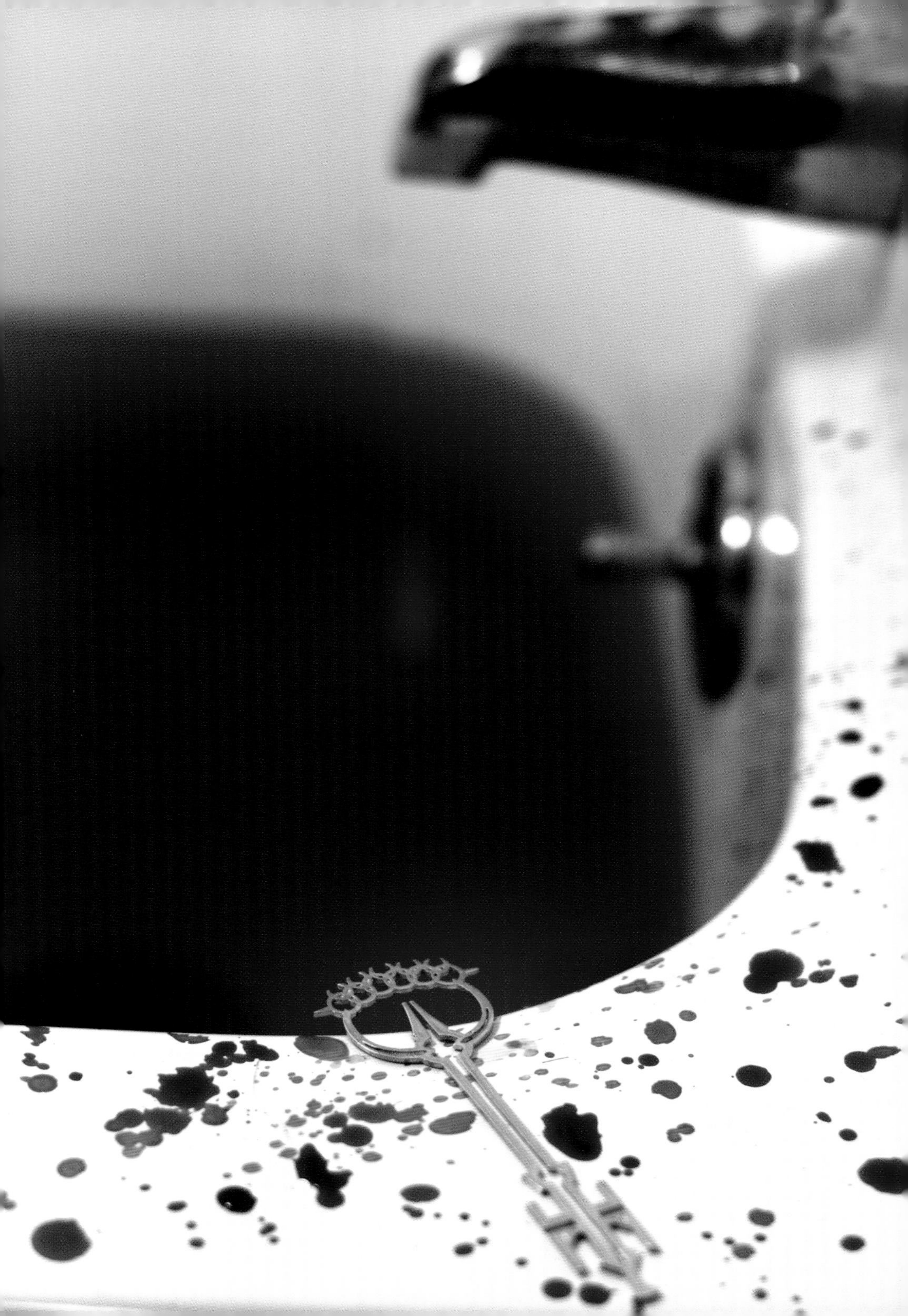

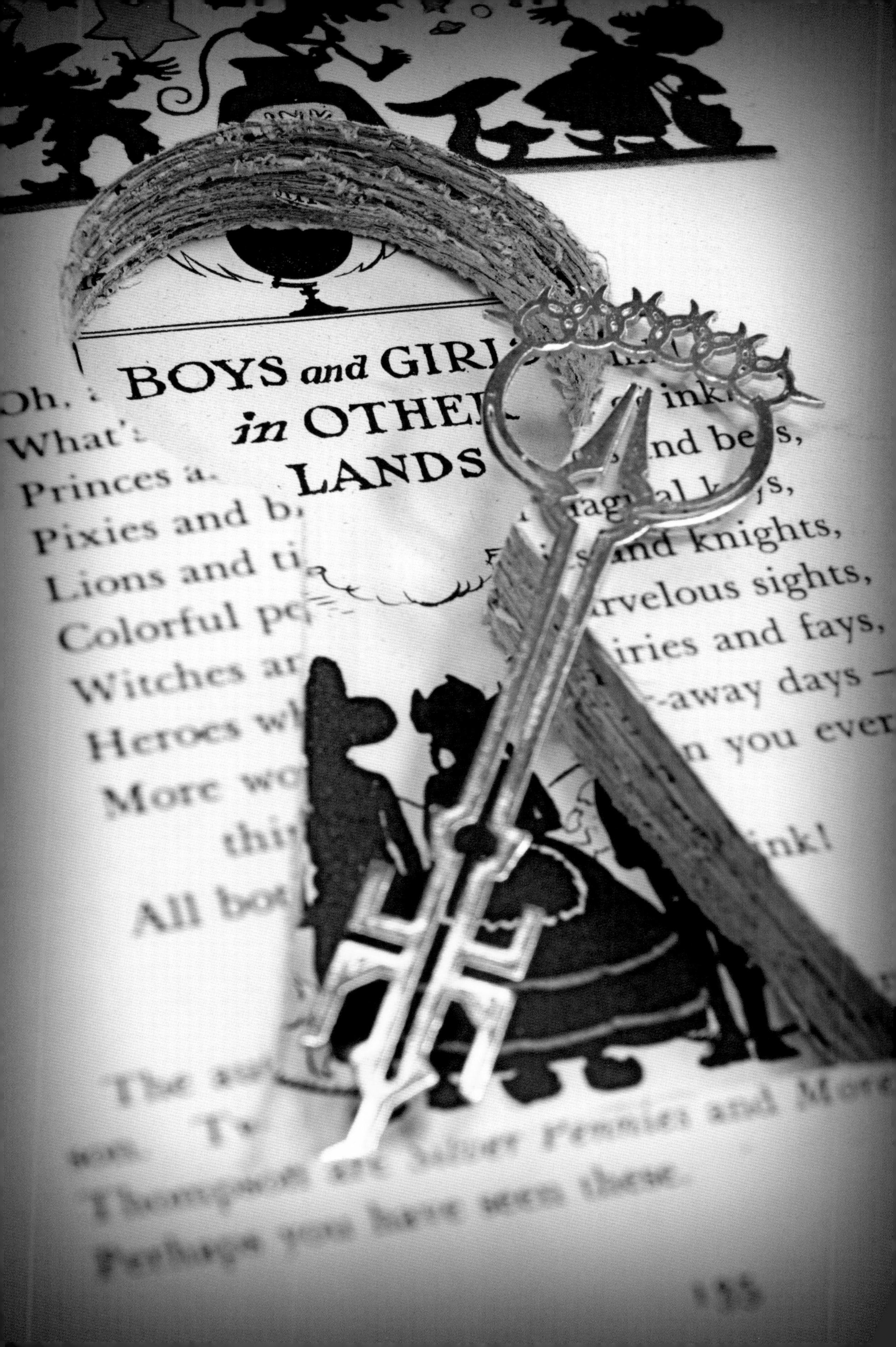
BOYS and
in
LANDS
Princes
Pixies and
Lions and
Colorful
Witches
Heroes
More
All
and knights,
rvelous sights,
iries and fays,
-away days —
you ever

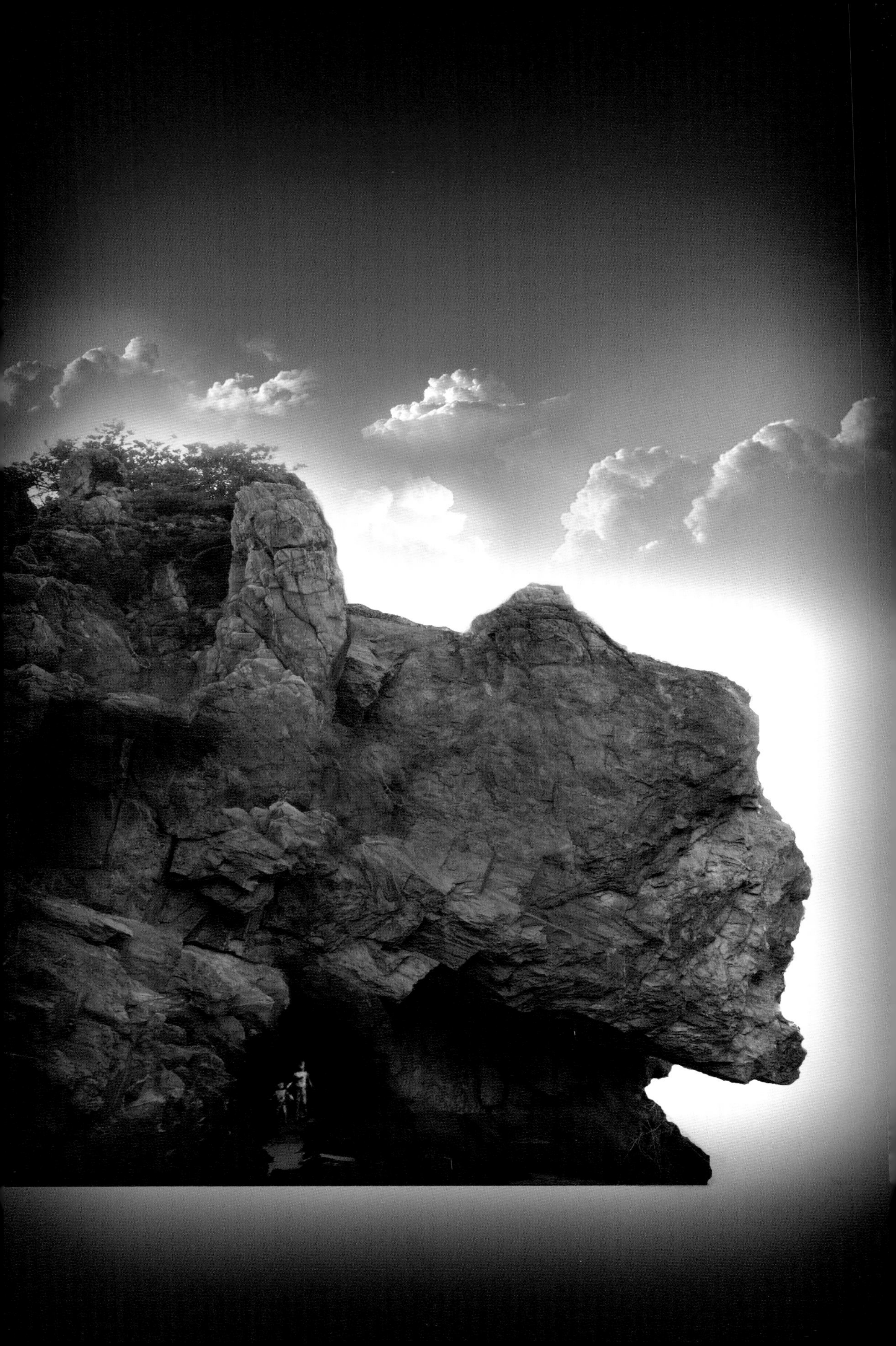

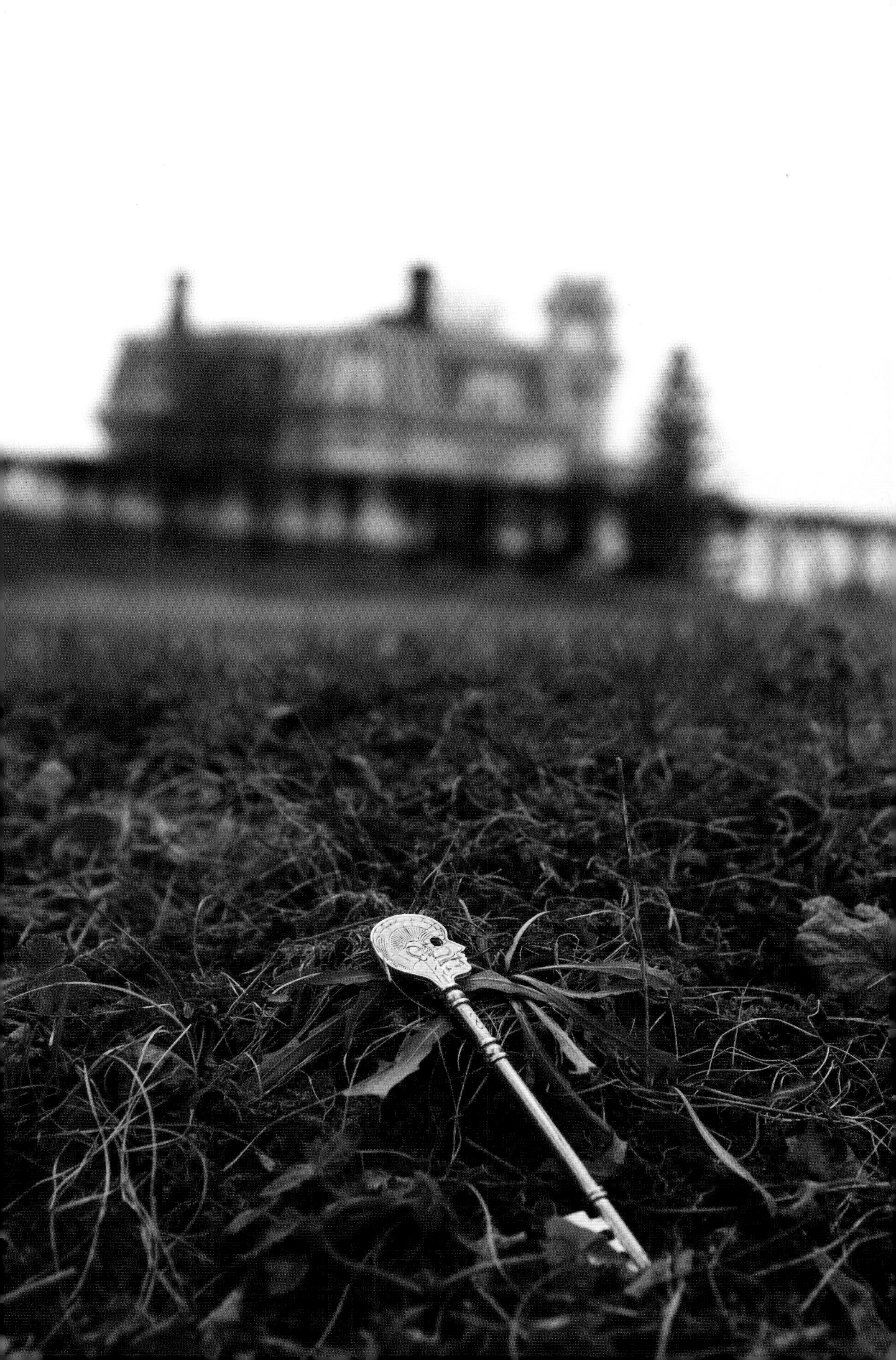

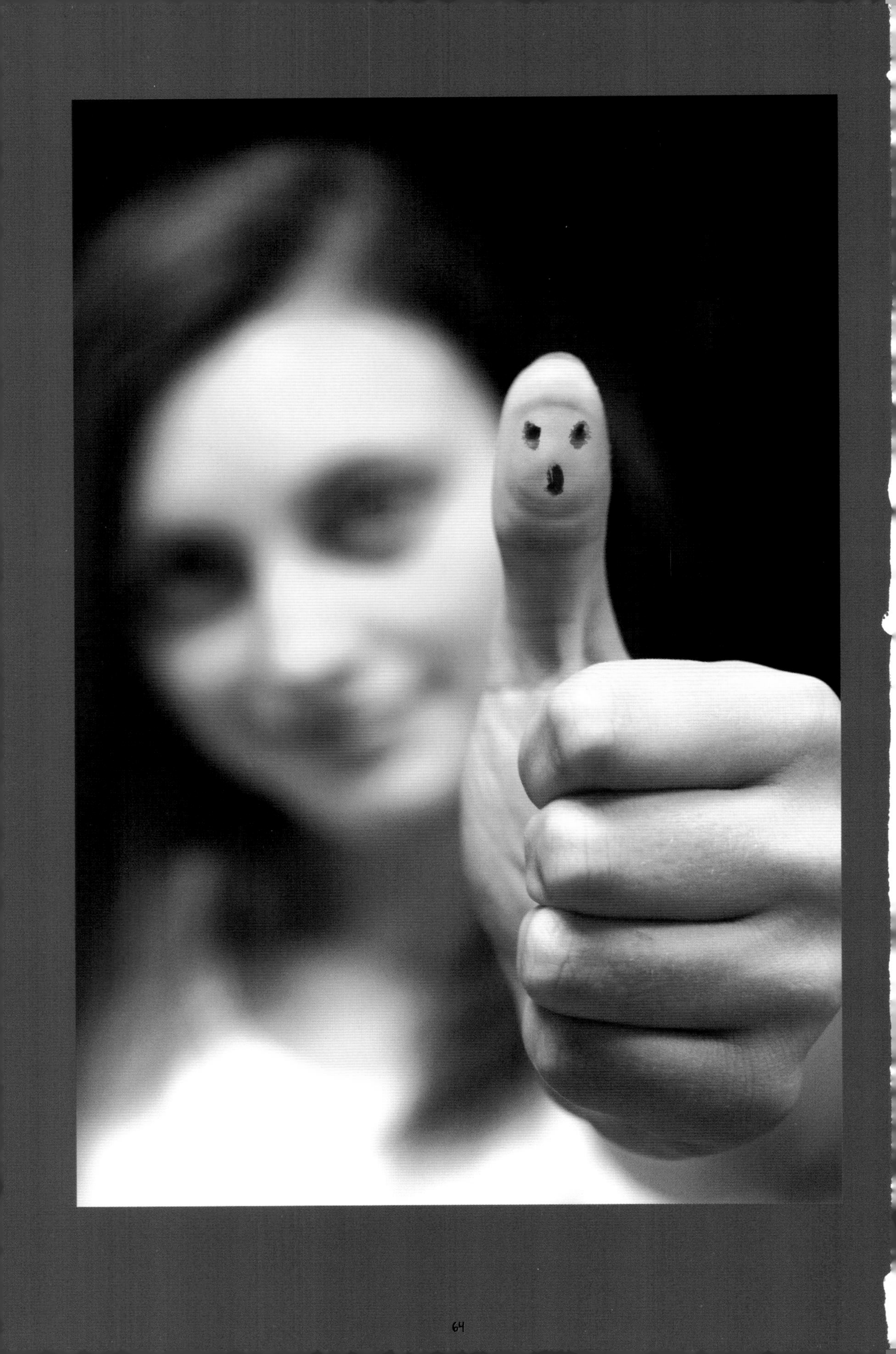

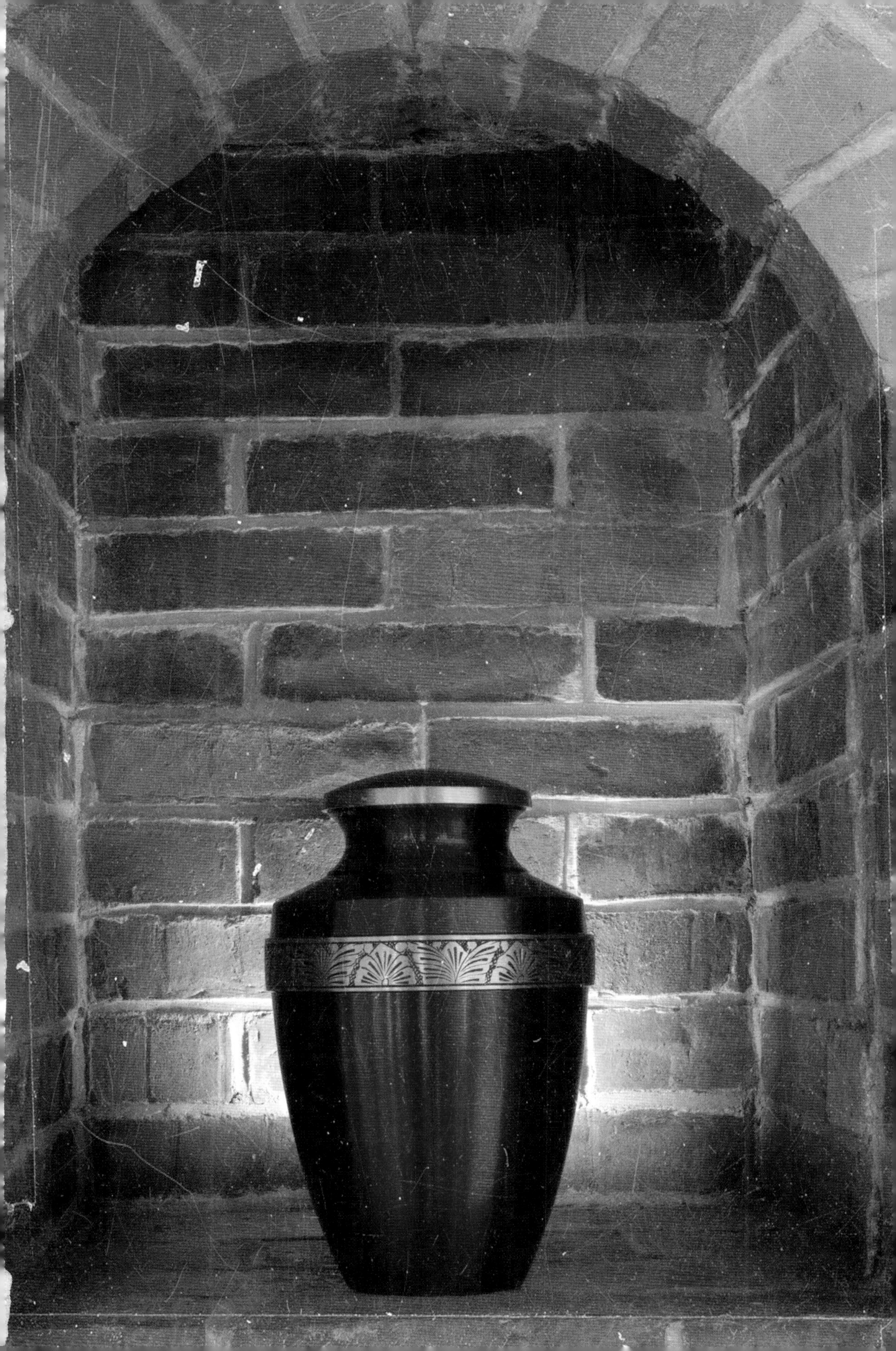

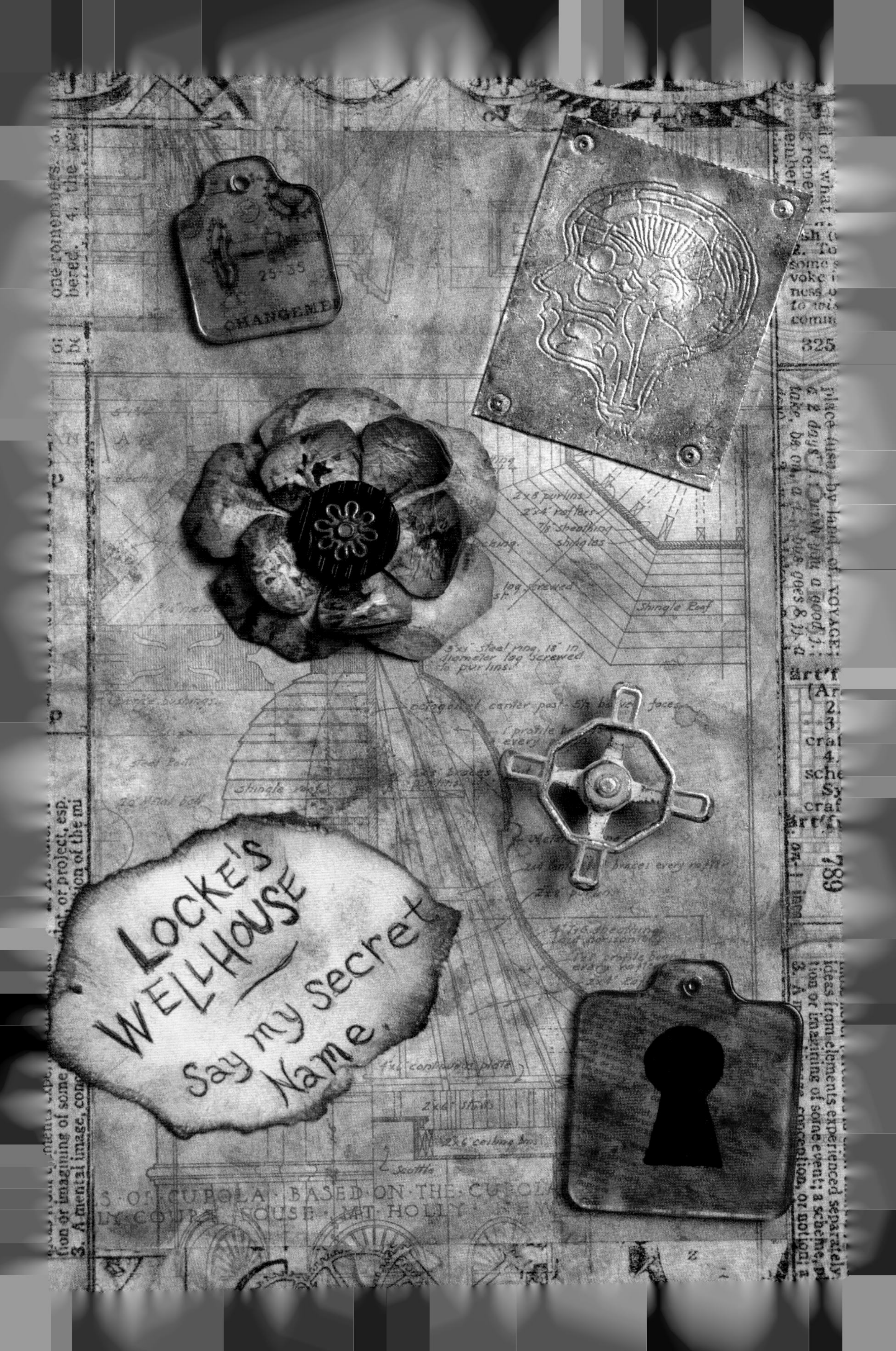
Locke's Wellhouse
Say my secret Name.

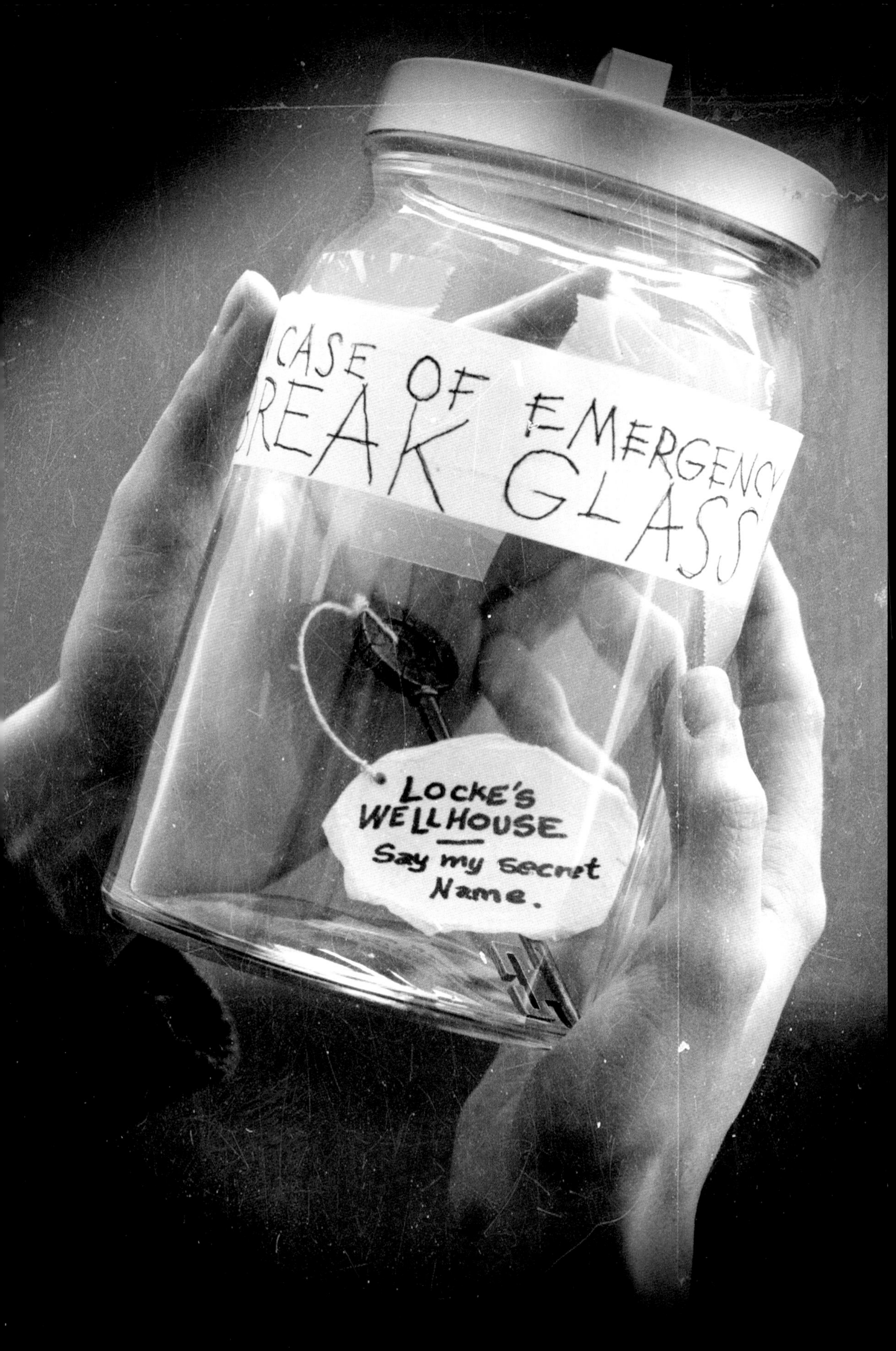
CASE OF EMERGENCY
REAK GLASS
LOCKE'S
WELLHOUSE
Say my secret
Name.

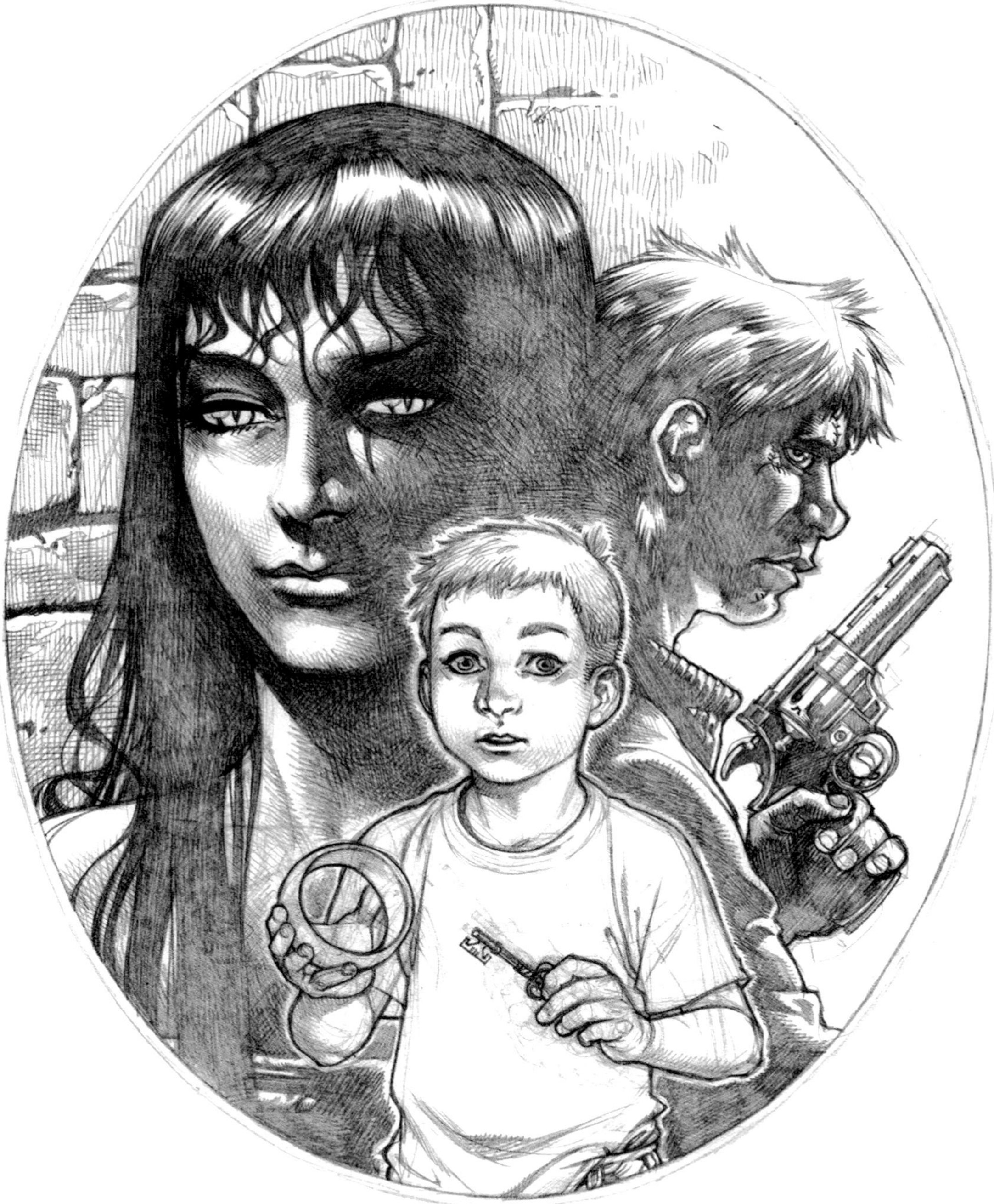

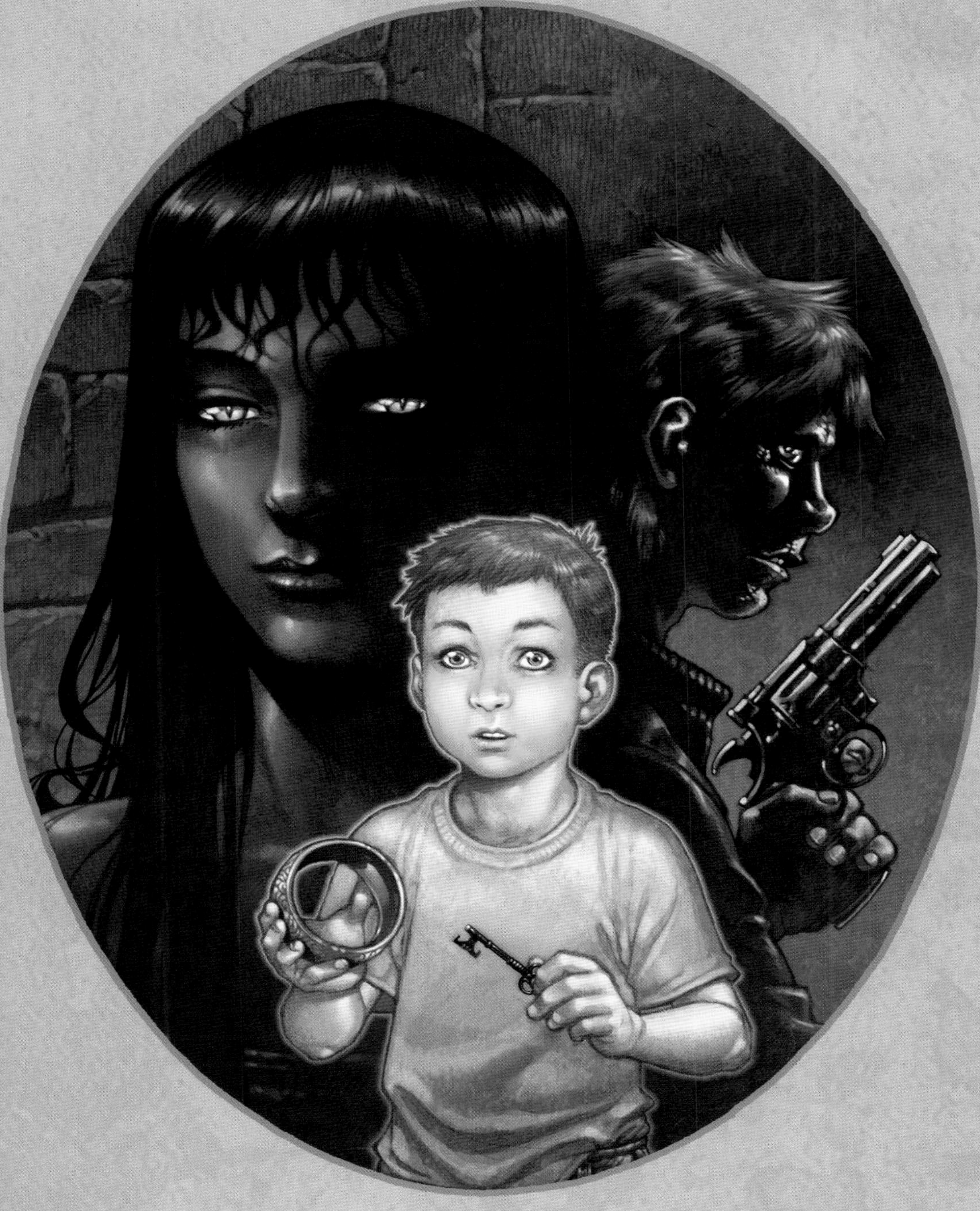

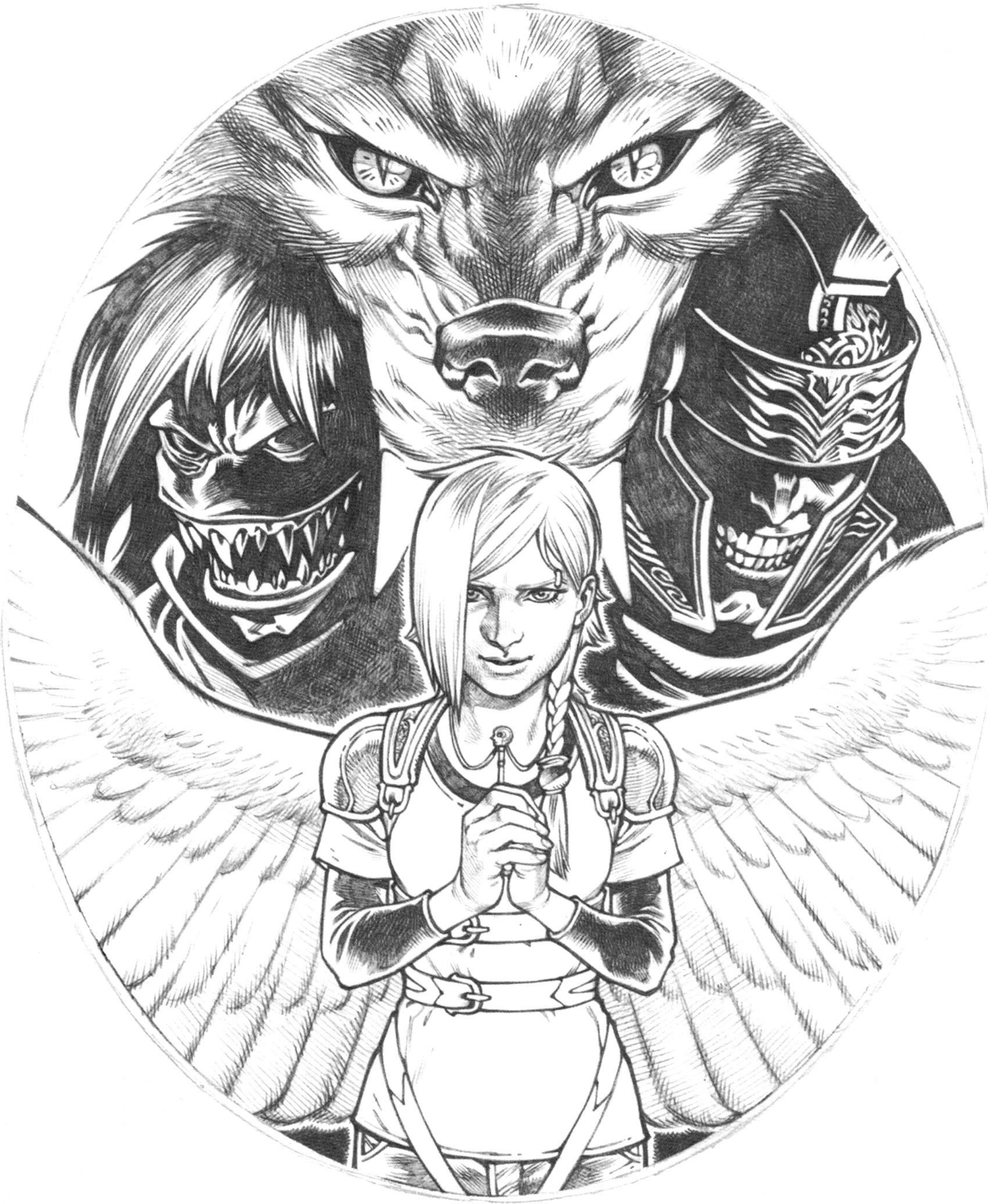

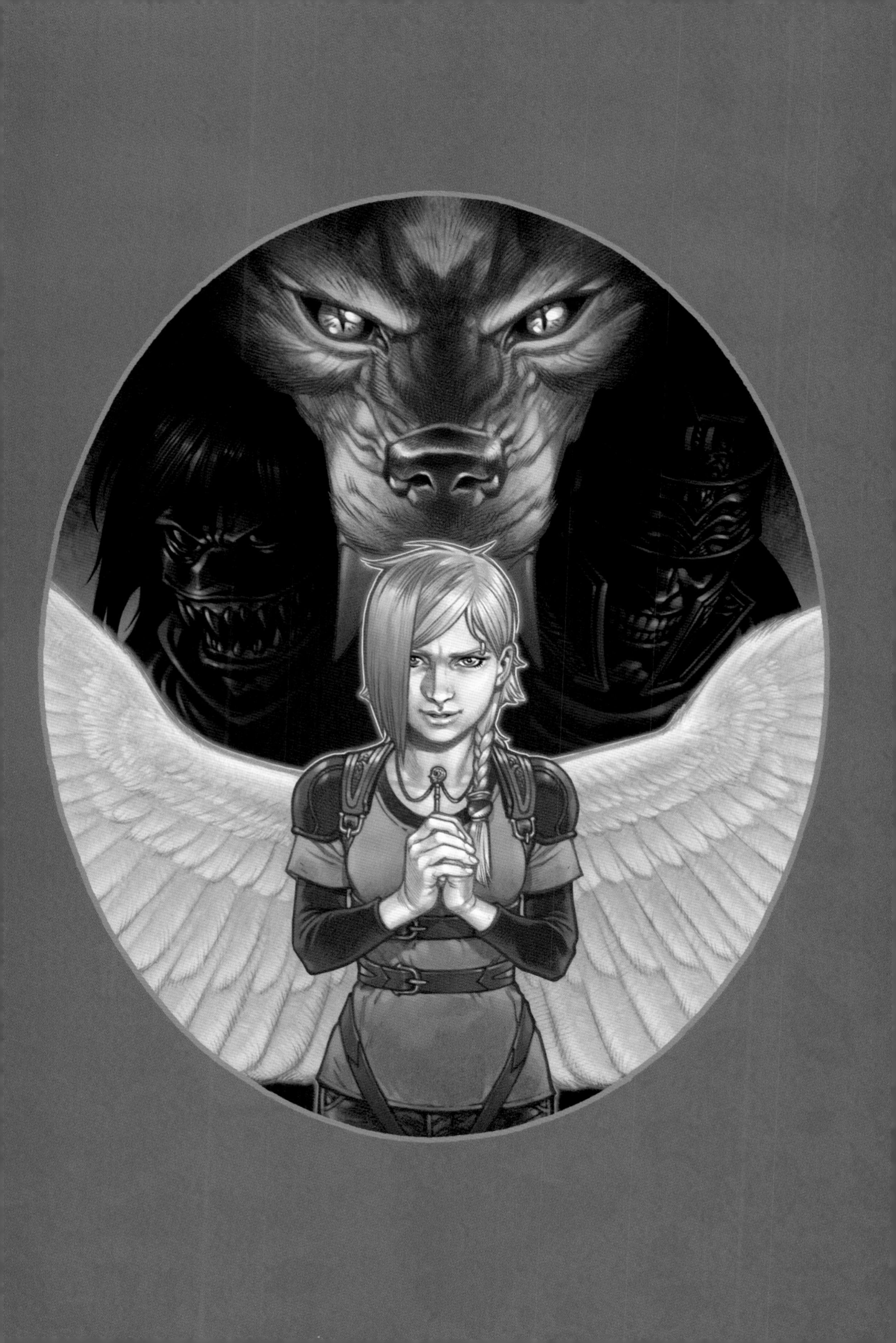

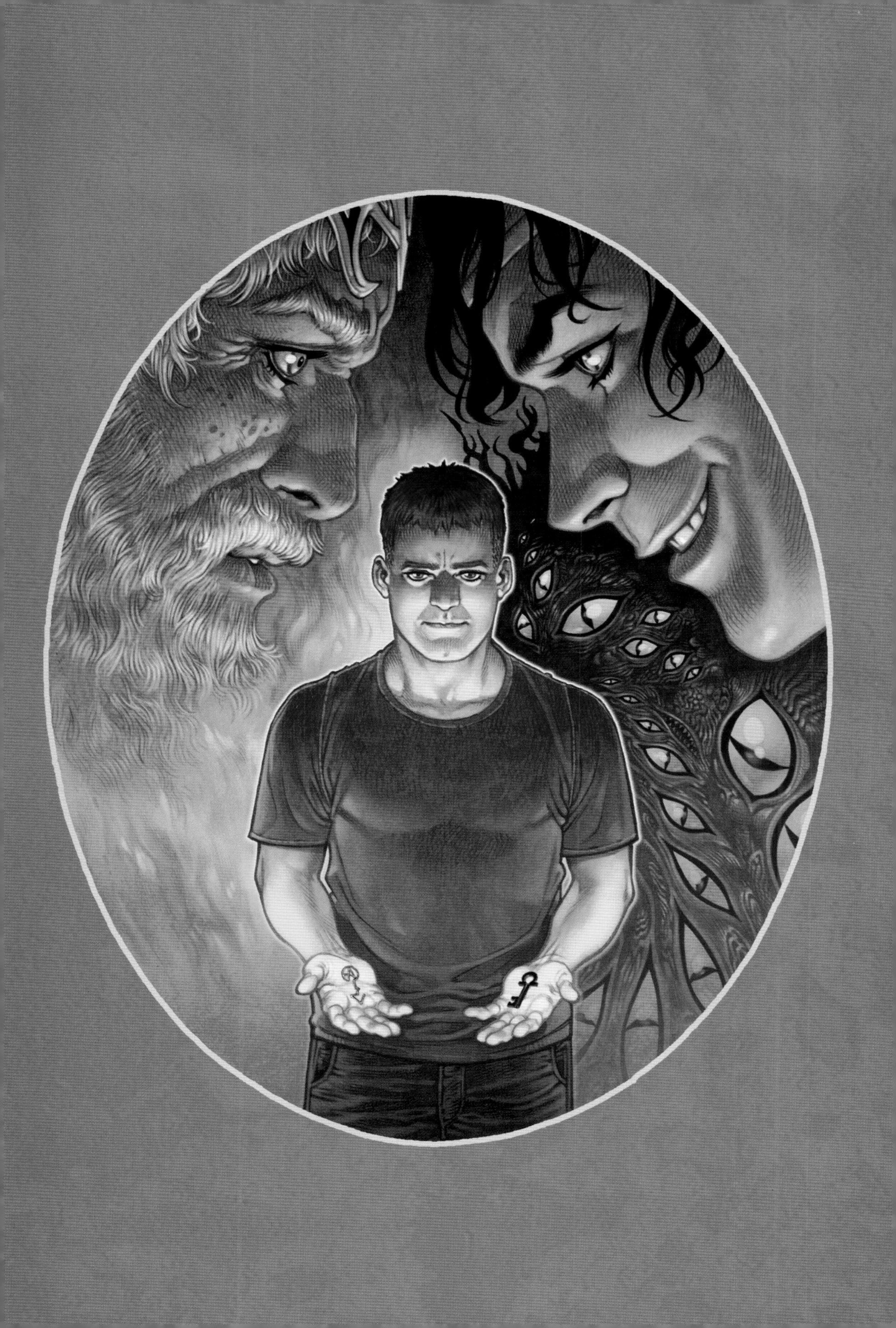

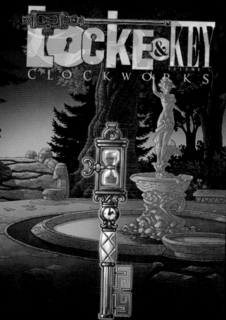
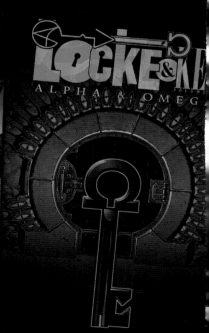